Introduction

Students are often uncertain as to what is required of them in preparation for the exams

This booklet:
- ✓ provides guidance for students specifically studying WJEC A2 Human Biology.
- ✓ is a study guide and you should build on the information provided by using diagrams obtained from textbooks.
- ✓ gives a good indication of the main points to be noted.
- ✓ gives a guide as to the depth of treatment required.

An active role in your studies

- In order to revise effectively it is important to take an **active role** in the process. Passive reading through your notes has limited value. The guide suggests '**Action points**' where you:
- ✓ draw labelled diagrams.
- ✓ draw graphs.
- ✓ analyse result tables.
- ✓ highlight key terms and provide definitions.
- ✓ construct comparison tables.
- ✓ describe processes using flowcharts/flow diagrams.
- This does not mean that these activities are the only ones that you should carry out in preparation for an exam. They are merely suggestions. There may, for example, be a number of other drawings that you should consider.

Revision hints

Examiners are aware that candidates are often not able to effectively show the examiner what they know.
To overcome this problem it is necessary to:
- ✓ devise a structured **revision programme**. Revise regularly - repetition is an important tool in learning and in preparing for exams. Revise each topic as soon as it is completed. Success is achieved through consistent work rather than attempting to commit everything to memory at the last minute.
- ✓ **understand basic principles** e.g. by learning definitions.
- ✓ **revise all topics**. Each unit will contain a number of structured questions with one essay question. It is not a good idea to work out which topics are 'going to come up'. Examiners take great care that the questions cover every topic.
- ✓ produce **annotated diagrams** – these are a good way of revising!
- ✓ familiarise yourself with **past exam questions**.
- ✓ **express yourself clearly and concisely** -frequently students, who know a reasonable amount of biology, don't do themselves justice in an exam because of their poor exam technique. Much of this is to do with the problem of language. It can make the difference between a good grade and an average grade. You need to be able to read, interpret, memorise, understand and convey information concisely in order to answer exam questions successfully.
- ✓ understand the **key words** that are used in exam questions.

It is hoped that the guide may prove of real value to the student.
The author is a principal examiner for WJEC and has written a further revision guide for the new specification 2008 together with a question book.

Revision express "A - level study guide Biology"
(Pearson Education ISBN 978-1-4082-0649-2)

Both publications complement the information in this booklet and provide an extension to the activities and information outlined here. This booklet, which emphasises the WJEC specific material, is largely, though not exclusively, based on the study guide.

Gareth Rowlands October 2008

Websites

www.revision-express.com

www.wjec.co.uk

4.2 Aerobic Respiration

Respiration is a series of enzyme catalysed reactions which release energy from organic molecules in order to synthesise ATP. Aerobic respiration, which requires oxygen, consists of four distinct but linked stages: glycolysis, the link reaction, Krebs Cycle, and the electron transport chain.

Glycolysis

Glycolysis takes place in the cytoplasm and oxygen is not required.
- The **glucose** molecule is first **phosphorylated** to make it more reactive by the addition of two molecules of ATP to form **hexose phosphate**.
- The 6-carbon hexose phosphate is split into two molecules of **triose phosphate** (3-carbon sugar).
- Each 3-carbon sugar is converted to **pyruvic acid**.
- Two of the steps transfer sufficient energy for the synthesis of ATP yielding a total of four ATP molecules. Since these are formed directly from phosphate compounds in the process it is known as **substrate level phosphorylation.**
- Thus, the breakdown of one molecule of glucose produces two molecules of ATP, two molecules of reduced NAD and two molecules of pyruvate.

Link reaction

- Pyruvic acid diffuses from the cytoplasm to the mitochondrial matrix.
- The two molecules of pyruvate (3-carbon) from glycolysis are converted to two molecules of 2-carbon acetate with the formation of two molecules of reduced NAD and the loss of two molecules of carbon dioxide.
- The acetate then combines with coenzyme A to form **acetyl coenzyme A.**

Krebs Cycle

1. The function of the Krebs cycle is a means of liberating energy from carbon bonds to provide ATP and reduced NAD (and FAD), with the release of carbon dioxide.
2. Reduced NAD (and FAD) deliver the hydrogen to the electron transport system in the inner mitochondrial membrane so acting as triggers for this system.

- The acetyl CoA then enters the Krebs cycle by combining with a 4-carbon acid, to form a 6-carbon compound, citric acid; the CoA is regenerated.
- The 6-carbon compound undergoes reactions during which carbon dioxide and hydrogen atoms are removed. After the acetate fragment is broken down, the remaining four carbon residue undergoes conversion to regenerate the four carbon compound which combines with more acetyl CoA.
- Two of the steps involve **decarboxylation,** and four of the steps involve **dehydrogenation**.
- The hydrogen atoms produced are collected by two different carriers with the formation of three molecules of NADH/H$^+$ (reduced NAD) and one molecule of FADH$_2$ (reduced FAD).
- Thus, for each turn of the cycle the overall production is one ATP, three reduced NAD and one reduced FAD. Since these are produced from the breakdown of one molecule of pyruvate, the two molecules produced in glycolysis will give double this yield.

Electron transport system

- Although the glucose molecule has been completely oxidised by the end of the Kreb's cycle, much of the energy is in the form of hydrogen atoms which are attached to the hydrogen acceptor molecules NAD and FAD.
- The hydrogen atoms split into their protons and electrons. The protons enter the space between the inner and outer membrane of the mitochondrion by the **proton pump** mechanism (see the previous section) while the electrons pass along the carriers and associated pumps, known as the **electron transport chain**, located within the inner membrane.
- It is the flow of protons back into the matrix via the stalked granules (due to their high concentration in the intermembrane space) that acts as the driving force to synthesise ATP.
- These protons then recombine in the matrix with the electrons, and the hydrogen atoms so formed then combine with oxygen to form water.
- If NADH is the initial acceptor, for each pair of hydrogen atoms involved enough energy is released for the synthesis of three molecules of ATP. If FADH replaces NADH as the first carrier only two molecules of ATP are produced.

For the breakdown of one molecule of glucose:

Glycolysis	Link reaction	Krebs cycle
2NADH + 2 ATP directly (net)	2NADH	6NADH + 2ATP directly 2FADH$_2$

Ten molecules of NADH are made and each molecule produces three ATP molecules giving 30 ATP's.
Two molecules of FADH$_2$ are made and each molecule produces two ATP molecules giving 4 ATP's.
Four ATP's are made directly (substrate level phosphorylation)
This gives a total of 38 molecules of ATP produced from each molecule of glucose.

Note that:
- *The names of the proton pumps and electron carriers in the electron transport system are **not** required.*
- *The names of the intermediates of glycolysis and Kreb's cycle are **not** required.*
- *You are **not** required to know the names of all the enzymes involved at each stage but you should know that dehydrogenase enzymes catalyse the removal of hydrogen atoms and decarboxylases catalyse the removal of carbon dioxide.*

- ☐ **Action**   1. Draw a diagram that summarises aerobic respiration.
    (Include only the names of those chemicals mentioned in bold above and use only the terms – 6C, 5C and 4C - in the Kreb's cycle).
    2. Insert the points of removal of carbon dioxide and hydrogen atoms.
    3. Show on your diagram that for each pair of hydrogen atoms evolved, three molecules of ATP are produced (except for one of the carrier systems in the Kreb's cycle where FAD replaces NAD as the first acceptor).
    4. Total the *net* gain of ATP molecules from one molecule of glucose.
    (Don't forget that 2ATP's are used in the phosphorylation of the glucose molecule and that you must double the number of ATP's produced by the Kreb's cycle because for each glucose molecule broken down, the cycle turns twice – once for each molecule of pyruvic acid produced). *This is dealt with in detail in the next section.*
    5. Make a list of key terms and write definitions for each.

Anaerobic Respiration, Energy Budgets

Anaerobic respiration occurs in some microorganisms and in some tissues, e.g. muscle cells which may be temporarily deprived of oxygen. However, without oxygen, oxidative phosphorylation will not take place and so the yield of ATP molecules will be greatly reduced. You need to be able to compare and explain the differences in yields of ATP from aerobic and anaerobic respiration.

Anaerobic respiration

In the absence of oxygen:
- Only the first stage of respiration, glycolysis, can take place.
- The reduced NAD (and FAD) cannot be reoxidised and therefore made available to pick up more hydrogen and so the link reaction and the Kreb's cycle cannot take place.
- The yield of ATP is greatly reduced.

In the matrix protons recombine with electrons to form hydrogen atoms which then combine with oxygen to form water. Since most of the yield of useful energy by metabolism comes from the transfer of hydrogen atoms or electrons, oxygen must be available to accept the hydrogen atom. If oxygen is absent the hydrogen atoms are not removed at the end of the respiratory chain and will accumulate. While oxygen only performs this function at the end of the many stages of respiration, it is nevertheless vital as it drives the whole process.

- In vertebrate muscle cells **lactic acid** is produced. The pyruvate itself becomes the hydrogen acceptor.
- In higher plants and yeast, **alcohol** is the product. This is also known as alcoholic fermentation.

Fermentation

Fermentation takes place in yeast when the pyruvate is converted to alcohol and carbon dioxide.
- The pyruvate is first decarboxylated to produce ethanal.
- The hydrogen released during glycolysis is passed on to NAD.
- The reduced NAD then passes the hydrogen to ethanal which is reduced to ethanol. Fermentation yields two molecules of ATP and this represents an efficiency of only 2%.

Lactic acid formation in muscle

During vigorous exercise the human body cannot get sufficient oxygen to the muscle cells. Instead of respiring aerobically the cells can only produce ATP by glycolysis.
- The reduced NAD produced during glycolysis passes its hydrogen directly to pyruvate, thus reducing it to lactate.
- Again, the process yields two molecules of ATP with a low energy release of 2%.

Build-up of lactic acid in muscle causes cramp. When oxygen becomes available again the lactic acid is broken down in the liver. Most is converted to glycogen and stored for further energy release.
The oxygen required to break down the lactate is called the oxygen debt. At the end of exercise the oxygen debt is repaid by deep and rapid breathing.

Remember that:

Usually 3 ATP molecules are produced every time 2 hydrogen atoms pass through the carrier system.

The energy yield for each molecule of reduced NAD is three ATP

The energy yield for each molecule of reduced FAD is two ATP

As there are two pyruvate molecules formed for each glucose molecule all figures for the link reaction and Kreb's cycle must be doubled (x2).

Glycolysis
2 ATP used (in the phosphorylation of glucose).
4 ATP produced directly (by substrate level phosphorylation).
6 ATP produced (from 2 pairs of H atoms picked up by NAD which may enter the mitochondrion and pass along the electron transport system).
8 ATP = net gain

Link reaction
(2x) 3 ATP
6 ATP

Krebs Cycle
(2 x) 1 ATP formed directly (by substrate level phosphorylation).
(2 x) 11 ATP from electron transport chain.
(three pairs of hydrogen atoms via NAD yields 9 ATP; one pair via FAD yields 2 ATP)
24 ATP = net gain from Krebs cycle
Total net gain = **38 ATP** molecules

Respiratory fuels

All living organisms require a continuous supply of energy for the various activities of the body. Glucose is broken down by means of enzymes through a number of intermediate compounds, with the controlled release of small quantities of energy at each stage. These reactions provide the energy to produce ATP. Muscle fibres, like all other body cells, produce their ATP through respiration. Respiration needs a source of fuel, such as glucose. However, glucose is not the only fuel that muscles can use.

Respiratory fuels

Muscles need ATP to contract. Resting muscle does not store much ATP and once used up more ATP must be produced. Like all cells, muscle cells produce ATP by the process of respiration. Fuels that provide energy in the body are referred to as 'respiratory substrates'. As well as glucose, lipids and amino acids can be broken down to produce ATP. These different respiratory substrates have different energy values. Carbohydrates and proteins release about $17kJg^{-1}$ whereas the value for fat is about twice this amount.

Different tissues in the body tend to use different substrates:
- glycogen stored in the muscle and liver is the first energy source used during exercise.
- as well as carbohydrates muscles also use fatty acids.
- blood glucose is used to supply the brain and nervous system.
- cardiac muscle gets about 70% of its ATP by using fatty acids.

Burning fuels to release ATP

During normal body activity fat provides an energy store and is used as a respiratory substrate when carbohydrate levels are low. Fat can be split into its constituent molecules of glycerol and fatty acids by hydrolysis. The two-carbon acetyl fragments combine with coenzyme A to form acetyl coenzyme A, which is fed into the Krebs cycle. The glycerol is phosphorylated into triose phosphate which is an intermediate in glycolysis. It is converted to pyruvate which is then broken down yielding ATP molecules in the Krebs cycle.

When proteins are used in respiration

A shortage or complete lack of food leads to starvation. People are able to survive for long periods without food as long as they have access to water. This is because they are able to use their reserves of carbohydrate, fat and protein to provide energy. As starvation proceeds the body uses;
- Liver glycogen stores - these last less than a day.
- Fat stores - these last between four to six weeks.
- Protein in muscles and other tissues – these last between one to two weeks.

Common symptoms of protein energy malnutrition are the conditions of wasting and stunting. Proteins are not stored so reserves are in the tissues themselves. Only if a person is starving is their tissue protein used as a source of energy, but a certain amount of energy is always derived from excess dietary protein.

In prolonged starvation the tissue protein is mobilised to supply energy and whenever dietary energy supplies are inadequate the protein component of the food is diverted for energy purposes. The protein is hydrolysed into its constituent amino acids. These are deaminated in the liver, with the removal of the NH2 group which is converted into urea and excreted. The residue can be fed into the Krebs cycle with the production of molecules of ATP.
Protein is very rarely used as a respiratory substrate, usually only when all reserves of carbohydrate and fat have been used up.

Muscles

Movements of the body are brought about by the contraction of voluntary muscles, which are attached to movable bones of the skeleton. Energy in the form of ATP is needed for the contraction of muscles. The sliding-filament theory explains how a muscle contracts. You should look at the structure of skeletal muscle as seen with the light and electron microscopes.

The structure of muscle

- An individual muscle consists of hundreds of **muscle fibres**. Each fibre is made up of a mass of parallel **myofibrils** running the length of the fibre. When viewed under the light microscope myofibrils show a pattern of alternate light and dark bands (known as I and A bands). Hence the alternative name for voluntary muscle is 'striped' or 'striated' muscle.

❑ *Action*   Draw voluntary muscle as seen under the light microscope.

- Seen under the electron microscope striated muscle consists of fibres, each of which is a long, multinucleate cell. The cell wall, or **sarcolemma**, encloses several nuclei, cytoplasm and numerous mitochondria.It also contains the contractile elements, which are long protein fibres, the myofibrils. Each myofibril is divided into **sarcomeres** by cross partitions, Z lines.
  In each sarcomere there are two types of protein:
  ✓ thin **actin** filaments projecting into the sarcomere from the Z lines.
  ✓ thicker **myosin** filaments between them, which are fixed in position by molecular bonds.

❑ *Action*   1.Draw the structure of a myofibril as seen under the electron microscope.
    (Show the arrangement of thin actin and thick myosin filaments;
    labels - sarcomere, Z line, A band (entire length of myosin filaments including
    overlap with actin), I band (actin only), H zone(myosin only), M line.
    2. Draw cross sections of the sarcomere at different points.

The sliding-filament theory of muscular contraction

This theory suggests that the muscle filaments do not shorten when the muscle contracts but that they slide between one another. The theory is based on the study of electron micrographs of muscles fixed at different degrees of tension. It appears that the actin filaments, and therefore the Z lines to which they are attached, are pulled towards each other, sliding as they do so over the myosin filaments.

Contraction mechanism
- When the muscle receives a nerve impulse the sarcomeres shorten due to increased overlap of the actin and myosin strands.
✓ H zone shortens
✓ I bands shorten
✓ Z lines become closer together (i.e. sarcomere shortens)
✓ A band does not change in length.
- The actin filaments slide over the myosin filaments with no change in length of either .

❑ *Action*   Draw diagrams to illustrate sliding-filament theory.

The 'ratchet mechanism' may be used to explain how the actin and myosin filaments slide past one another.

✓ When an impulse reaches the neuromuscular junction acetylcholine is released which causes the sarcolemma of the muscle to be depolarised. This causes the release of calcium ions which activate the protein **troponin**. This displaces another protein, **tropomyosin** (which has been blocking the actin filament) away from attachment sites on the actin molecule so myosin and actin can be linked by cross bridges.
✓ The bulbous heads along the myosin filaments form these bridges.
✓ Each myosin filament has a number of bulbous heads.
✓ The clubbed heads of the myosin molecule swing back and forth with the breaking and reforming of bonds.
✓ The bulbous heads progressively moves the actin filaments along as they become attached and detached.
✓ The process receives energy by the hydrolysis of ATP.

❏ *Action*   Explain the ratchet mechanism by means of annotated diagrams.

The neuromuscular junction

What makes a muscle contract?
Striated muscle must be stimulated by an impulse from a motor nerve. The point where the motor nerve meets a striated muscle is called the **neuromuscular junction** or end plate.
The structure of a neuromuscular junction is similar to a synaptic knob and the post synaptic membrane is greatly folded to form a motor end-plate.

❏ **Action**   Draw a labelled diagram of a neuromuscular junction.

When a nerve impulse is received at the end plate the sequence of events is much the same as the mechanism of synaptic transmission.

❏ **Action**   Describe the sequence of events which occur at the end plate.

Muscle types and athletes

It is generally accepted that muscle fibres can be broken down into two main types: **slow twitch (Type I)** muscle fibres and **fast twitch (Type II)** muscle fibres. Human muscles contain a genetically determined mixture of both slow and fast fibre types. On average, humans have about 50 percent slow twitch and 50 percent fast twitch fibres in most of the muscles used for movement.

Many people believe that the relative number of fast and slow twitch muscle fibres may determine what sports athletes excel at and how they respond to training. This may be due to the fact that each fibre type is unique in its ability to contract in a certain way.

Slow Twitch (Type I)
The slow muscles are more efficient at using oxygen to generate more ATP for continuous, extended muscle contractions over a long time. They fire more slowly than fast twitch fibres and can act for a long time before they fatigue. Therefore, slow twitch fibres are great at helping athletes run marathons.

Fast Twitch (Type II)
As fast twitch fibres use anaerobic metabolism to create ATP, they are much better at generating short bursts of strength or speed than slow muscles. However, they fatigue more quickly. Fast twitch fibres generally produce the same amount of force per contraction as slow twitch fibres but they get their name because they are able to fire more rapidly. Having a greater number of fast twitch fibres can be an asset to a sprinter since he or she needs to quickly generate a lot of force.

Can Training Change Fibre Type?
This is not entirely understood and research is continuing in this area. There is some evidence to show that human skeletal muscle may switch fibre types from "fast" to "slow" due to training.

Respiration and athletic performance

To enable muscles to contract a source of energy in the form of ATP is produced during respiration. Only a limited amount of ATP is present in muscle cells; sufficient to allow a person to run quickly for a few seconds. Once used up more ATP must be produced.

ATP is created in two ways:

- During high intensity exercise, ATP is provided by anaerobic respiration which does not require an ongoing supply of oxygen. Anaerobic pathways can provide ATP immediately but they also have limited stores that need to be refilled after they are used up.

- During aerobic respiration the remaining energy available in glucose is released using oxygen carried in the bloodstream. Aerobic respiration involves the Krebs cycle and the electron transport chain. This process takes longer than glycolysis but has the advantage of releasing a considerable quantity of energy. However, there is a limit on how fast aerobic respiration can work. This is because the cardiovascular system is limited in its ability to quickly deliver blood and oxygen to the working muscles.
  The aerobic system is essential for endurance events.

During exercise, glycogen, rather than fat, is the main energy source because glycogen needs less oxygen to break it down. However, as glycogen is in limited supply the body needs to use some fat to conserve glycogen. Training programmes for endurance athletes help the body to use more fat reserves enabling the body to be less reliant on glycogen.

Athletes wanting to increase their performance will try to store as much energy as possible in their muscle cells. These stores can be used to produce ATP much faster than if the muscles had to rely on glucose supplied in the blood.

Another technique practised by endurance athletes is carbohydrate loading. This method increases the athlete's muscle glycogen stores. Before a race, an athlete follows a regime of a few days of hard exercise while eating foods containing a lot of carbohydrate, e.g. pasta. The carbohydrate is broken down to glucose in the digestive system and absorbed into the blood. Some of this glucose is taken into the muscle fibres and converted to glycogen for storage. It is important to realise that carbohydrate loading cannot help the muscles to work harder or faster but enables them to work for longer. It is only beneficial for endurance athletes.

Lactic acid and exercise

During intense exercise, such as sprinting or lifting heavy weights, muscles rely on anaerobic metabolism, which can only produce a certain amount of energy for a limited time, unlike the aerobic metabolism system, which can produce energy over a long period of time (hours).

Training can make a difference in how long and fast both of the metabolic pathways work. Trained athletes have a greater ability to quickly deliver oxygen to the working muscles which increases the ability to use aerobic metabolism at a higher exercise intensity. Trained athletes also develop a greater efficiency in energy delivery. Finally training may improve the way the body creates and uses the anaerobic systems so you can access ATP more readily.

During vigorous exercise anaerobic respiration takes place and the pyruvate is converted to lactate. There is a build-up of lactic acid in the muscles causing fatigue and cramp.

The oxygen debt

Muscles need oxygen and an energy source such as glucose to provide them with the energy needed for contraction. If oxygen is not supplied to the muscles in sufficient quantity then some energy is provided by anaerobic respiration but not for very long because lactic acid builds up. This build up of lactic acid stops the muscles working.

The lactate diffuses into the blood and is carried to the liver where it is converted back to pyruvate when oxygen becomes available again. The pyruvate can then enter the link reaction. The removal of lactate by the liver after exercise requires extra oxygen. Consider an athlete running a 400 metre race. During most of the race the athlete's muscles will have been using oxygen at a faster rate than it can be supplied to them. The difference between the oxygen demand of the muscles and the oxygen they receive is called the **oxygen debt**. At the end of the race, heart rate and breathing rate continue at a high level to supply the oxygen needed to the liver to remove the lactate that has accumulated. This is sometimes referred to as 'paying back the oxygen debt' or, more correctly, it is called 'the excessive post-exercise oxygen consumption'.

Muscles respire anaerobically during short, fast periods of exercise. Training programmes improve blood supply to muscles, so that they can work longer and harder before they have to switch to anaerobic respiration. Long, steady runs improve cardiac output and the efficiency of oxygen uptake by the lungs. Training also increases the athlete's tolerance to the build-up of lactate in the tissues.
Endurance training increases the ability of the heart and lungs to get oxygen to the muscles as fast as possible over a long period of time.

4.3 Photosynthesis

The process of photosynthesis takes place in the chloroplasts. These are found in the mesophyll cells and guard cells of green leaves. In the chloroplasts the energy of sunlight is trapped by the pigment chlorophyll. At this stage you should review the structure of the leaf in unit 1, in particular the structure of the chloroplast. The biochemical process of photosynthesis may be divided into two parts, the light stage and the light independent stage. The light-dependent stage takes place in the thylakoid membrane of the chloroplast. It involves the photolysis of water and results in the production of ATP and reduced NADP with the release of oxygen as a waste product. The light-independent stage or Calvin cycle takes place in the stroma of the chloroplast. Here carbon dioxide combines with a 5-carbon acceptor and the products of the light-dependent stage are used to produce glucose.

The light dependent stage

1. The production of ATP
Chlorophyll is a pigment found in the thylakoid membranes of the chloroplast
When light hits a chlorophyll molecule:
- Some of the energy in the light is transferred to electrons in the chlorophyll.
- The 'excited' or 'energised' electrons are raised to a higher energy level and are picked up by an electron acceptor.
- The electron acceptor passes the electrons down a chain of carriers held in the membranes inside the chloroplast.
- This is similar to the electron transfer chain in respiration and as the electrons pass along the chain, energy is released from them and used to make ATP.
- Some of the sunlight energy is now trapped as chemical energy in an ATP molecule.
- This form of synthesis of ATP from ADP and Pi is called photophosphorylation.

2. The production of reduced NADP
- Sunlight also causes the splitting of water molecules, called photolysis.
- During photolysis the water molecule dissociates into electrons, hydrogen ions and oxygen.
    - ✓ The electrons replace those lost from the chlorophyll molecule.
    - ✓ The hydrogen ions combine with electrons released at the end of the chain of carriers and are picked up by NADP to give reduced NADP (NADPH).
    - ✓ Oxygen is released as a waste product.

Textbooks differ in their use of the term 'reduced NADP'. Some use $NADPH_2$, others $NADPH^+H^+$ (the latter being the accepted terminology used by the Biochemical Society in their booklet 'Biochemistry across the school curriculum'). Throughout this section the term 'reduced NADP' will be used.)

Light independent stage

The light independent stage occurs in the stroma of the chloroplast and involves many reactions each catalysed by a different enzyme. The reactions use the products of the light dependent stage, ATP as a source of energy, and reduced NADP as the source of the reducing power to reduce carbon dioxide and synthesise hexose sugar.

The sequence of events in this stage of photosynthesis was worked out by Calvin and his associates using C^{14}, a radioisotope of carbon, and the unicellular algae, *Chlorella*. It is known as the Calvin cycle.

- A five-carbon acceptor molecule, **ribulose bisphosphate (RuBP)**, combines with carbon dioxide (catalysed by the enzyme Rubisco) forming an unstable six-carbon compound.
- The six-carbon compound immediately splits into two molecules of a three-carbon compound called **glycerate-3-phosphate** (GP).
- GP is phosphorylated by ATP and **then** reduced by reduced NADP (from the light dependent stage) to **triose phosphate**.
- Some of this three-carbon sugar can be built up into glucose phosphate and then into starch by condensation.
- In order that the cycle continues, most of the triose phosphate formed enters a series of reactions, driven by ATP, which results in the regeneration of RuBP.

❏ *Action*   Draw a diagram to summarise the light independent stage.

Products of photosynthesis

The plant must synthesise all organic materials from the intermediates and products of photosynthesis. About one sixth of the triose phosphate produced by the Calvin cycle is used to synthesise glucose, lipids and amino acids.
- ✓ Glucose will be used in respiration.
- ✓ Glucose will be built up into long molecules of cellulose to form cell walls.
- ✓ Some will be made into lipids and used to make cell membranes or to provide food store in seeds such as olive oil.
- ✓ Some will be made into amino acids and then proteins, with the addition of nitrogen obtained from nitrates absorbed from the soil.

(You are **not** required to provide chemical details of these processes.)

❏ *Action*   Research the variety of plant structures used to provide food for other living organisms, including humans.

4.4 Microbiology

Microorganisms include Bacteria, Fungi, Viruses and Protoctista. This section describes the classification, growth and methods of counting bacteria. Particular emphasis is placed on the principles of aseptic technique. The principles involved in the batch culture fermenter are studied together with its application in the production of the antibiotic penicillin on a commercial scale.

Bacteria

Bacteria and fungi are extremely important in decaying dead organisms and thereby recycling nutrients. Certain bacteria, viruses and fungi can cause disease in humans, crops and domestic animals. This section deals in particular with bacteria. These are the smallest cellular organisms and are prokaryotes. The kingdom includes both heterotrophic and autotrophic forms.
There are several **ways of classifying bacteria**.
- One way is by their **shape**. Bacteria may be:
✓ **Bacillus** or rod shaped.
✓ **Cocci** or spherical.
✓ **Spirillum** or corkscrew shaped.

❑ *Action*　　　　Review the structure of a typical bacterial cell.

Further differentiation is often possible according to the way bacteria tend to be grouped e.g. in pairs; forming chains; in clusters. The filamentous bacteria are of particular interest because most are photosynthetic. This group, formerly called blue-green algae, are now known as Cyanobacteria.

- The **Gram stain** reaction enables microbiologists to distinguish between two types of bacteria. Bacteria are either Gram-positive or Gram-negative. The different staining properties are due to differences in the chemical composition of their cell walls.

    The cell wall consists of a mixture of polysaccharide and poypeptides, known as peptidoglycan or murein. The cross-linking provides strength, gives the cell its shape, and the wall protects against swelling and bursting (lysis) due to osmosis.

    Gram negative bacteria have more chemically complex walls where the peptidoglycan is supplemented by large molecules of lipopolysaccharide which protect the cell. They do not retain dyes like crystal violet. Gram-negative bacteria include *Salmonella* species. They are not affected by the antibacterial enzyme, lysozyme, which occurs in human tears, and are resistant to penicillin.

    Gram positive bacteria lack the lipopolysaccharide in their walls and do retain crystal violet. These are more susceptible to antibiotics and the enzyme, lysozyme, than gram negative bacteria. Gram-positive bacteria include *Bacillus, Staphylococcus and Streptococcus* species.

    (Penicillin kills bacteria by interfering with the ability to synthesise the cell wall. The bacteria are unable to divide and eventually the weakened cell wall ruptures.)

Bacteria reproduce asexually by **binary fission** although certain bacteria can also reproduce sexually. Some bacteria are pathogens and some cause deterioration of stored food, but it is important to remember that many are beneficial to humans.

Bacterial growth

There are four main phases of growth:
1. The lag phase, where there is little growth but the cells are taking up water and are carrying out protein synthesis and producing enzymes.
2. The exponential or log phase, where the population increases rapidly.
3. The stationary phase, where bacterial cells are dying at the same rate as they are produced.
4. The death phase, where more bacterial cells are dying than are being produced.
   (The phases of growth are dealt with in more detail in section 4.5 of this unit).

Conditions necessary for growth

Microorganisms reproduce quickly given a suitable environment. For example, bacteria are able to divide every twenty minutes under optimum conditions. In the laboratory bacteria can be grown on a wide variety of substrates providing they are supplied with suitable physical conditions, nutrients and water. Microrganisms vary in their requirements and usually grow over a range of temperatures and pH values, with an optimum within the range.

Microorganisms require the following conditions for growth:
- **Nutrients** – in the laboratory nutrients are supplied in nutrient media, such as agar, and include carbon, usually in the form of glucose; nitrogen, in organic and inorganic form; growth factors such as vitamins and mineral salts. Nitrogen is needed to produce amino acids during protein synthesis.
- **Temperature** – as all growth is normally regulated by enzymes the range of 25-45°C is favourable for the majority of bacteria. The optimum for mammalian pathogens is around 37° C.
- **pH** – most bacteria are favoured by slightly alkaline conditions (pH 7.4) (*whereas fungi prefer neutral to slightly acid conditions*).
- **Oxygen** – many microorganisms require oxygen for metabolism and are termed **obligate aerobes**. Some, while growing better in the presence of oxygen, can nevertheless survive in its absence; these are called **facultative anaerobes**. Others cannot grow in the presence of oxygen and are called **obligate anaerobes**. *Clostridium* bacteria are obligate anaerobes that produce toxins or poisons in a wound. These bacteria destroy body tissue and the condition is called moist gangrene.

4.4 Growth and culture techniques

All bacterial cultures are potentially dangerous. Samples should never be taken from surfaces in the laboratory. Cultures purchased from a scientific supplier, milk or yoghurt, are normally provided to carry out experimental work. There are two possible problems which must be prevented when working with bacteria. These are the prevention of contamination of the supplied cultures **from** the environment and the prevention of contamination **to** the environment. Strict safety precautions should be taken and aseptic techniques used at all times.

Aseptic technique

Bacteria (*and fungi*) are cultured (grown) on, or in, media that are designed to supply the cell with all its nutritional requirements. **Aseptic** techniques (also known as sterile techniques) in which the apparatus and equipment are kept free of microorganisms, are used to prevent contamination of bacterial cultures and the surrounding environment.

- **To prevent** the **contamination** of pure cultures and apparatus by bacteria **from** the **environment**:
- ✓ Sterilise all apparatus and media before use to prevent initial contamination.
- ✓ Handle cultures carefully and use equipment such as sterile loops to prevent subsequent contamination.
- **To prevent contamination to the environment** by the bacteria being used in experiments:
- ✓ Sterilise the work surface before and after an experiment using a disinfectant, e.g. Lysol used as a 3% solution.
- ✓ Use the **correct handling techniques** to prevent the contamination of personnel and the immediate environment by the organisms being cultured.
  For example, when carrying out the process of inoculation:
- ▪ Grasp the culture bottle in one hand; remove the cap with the little finger of the other hand – do not place the cap down on the work surface.
- ▪ Flame the mouth of the bottle for 2 or 3 seconds.
- ▪ Pass the inoculating loop through a flame until red hot.
- ▪ Lift the lid of the petri dish just enough to allow entry of the inoculating loop.
- ▪ Secure the petri dish lid with adhesive tape. Use two pieces of tape to fasten the lid, but do not seal all the way round (as this could create anaerobic conditions and encourage the growth of possible pathogenic microorganisms).
- ▪ Incubate at around 25^0C (cultures should not be cultured at 37^0C as this is an ideal temperature for the growth of many pathogenic species).
- ▪ Do not open petri dishes after incubation.
- ✓ In a laboratory the preferred method of sterilisation is to use an **autoclave**. This is a sealed container in which glass and metal equipment is heated at 121^0C in steam under pressure for 15 minutes after the required pressure has been reached. This ensures that any resistant endospores are destroyed e.g. gram positive bacteria such as *Clostridium* are resistant to boiling.
  Disposable materials, such as plastic Petri dishes, can be sealed inside autoclavable plastic bags and placed in a dustbin after having been autoclaved.
- ✓ Radiation e.g. gamma rays, is used commercially to sterilise plastic equipment.

- ❏ *Action*   1. Make a list of all the terms used in microbiology e.g. inoculation, media, sterilisation etc. and write out the definitions of each term.
       2. Describe how you would safely obtain a pure culture of one species of bacterium from a culture containing a mixed bacterial suspension in a nutrient medium.

Methods of measuring growth

Estimating the growth of bacteria is extremely important. Environmental health officers regularly inspect food premises and take samples for analysis. Water boards check water supplies daily. Many products are produced using bacteria grown in fermenters. Measuring their growth is an important part of the process.

➤ The size of a population of microorganisms in liquid culture may be measured by counting cells directly, or by taking some indirect method such as the turbidity (cloudiness) of the culture.

Direct cell counts may be divided into:
✓ **total counts**, which include both living and dead cells.
✓ **viable counts**, which count living cells only.

➤ In practice, it is never possible to count whole populations of microorganisms. Instead, the cells in a very small **sample** of culture are counted, and the result multiplied up to give a population density in organisms per cm^3 of culture. Even then, the population density is likely to be so high that cell counts are usually made in known dilutions of the culture, usually in 10-fold steps. This is known as **serial dilution**.

There are several different methods of measuring growth:
• Rough estimates of growth rates can be made by regularly measuring the diameter of a bacterial or fungal colony as it spreads from a central point to cover the surface of a solid growth medium. This is known as the **dilution plating** technique.
A culture medium, such as milk, is made into a series of dilutions using the serial dilution technique.
✓ A sample, $1cm^3$, is streaked onto a sterile agar plate which is then placed in an incubator at 25°C for two days. After all the streaks have been allowed to grow, the dilution at which the colonies are distinct and separate is counted. (If the dilution is insufficient then colonies will merge, referred to as 'clumping', and counting is inaccurate). The separate colonies of bacteria are counted with the assumption being made that each colony has arisen from a single cell, which has divided asexually, from the original medium. To find the total viable cell count the number of colonies is multiplied by the appropriate dilution factor. This method makes no allowance for clumping of cells so may cause an underestimate of numbers.

• A more accurate method involves using a **haemocytometer**. This is a specialised microscope slide originally used to count red blood cells. Using the haemocytometer gives **total cell counts** as it is not possible to distinguish between living and dead cells. (You are not required to describe or use a haemocytometer.)

✓ A third method, known as **turbidimetry,** involves using a colorimeter to measure the cloudiness or turbidity of the culture as cell numbers increase. Results are derived by comparison with a standard graph of light absorbance plotted against known cell numbers. (You are not required to describe or use a calorimeter).

Fermenters

Biotechnology may be defined as the industrial application of biological processes. Industrial fermentation is widely used to culture bacterial and fungal cells.

There are a number of advantages to using microorganisms in fermentation.

The microbes grow rapidly and enzymes do not have to be supplied. This means that fermentation can take place at lower temperatures than normally used in industrial processes and therefore production is cheaper.

An important use of large scale industrial fermentation is the production of antibiotics such as penicillin.

Fermenter design

The following describes the main principles of batch fermentation:

- A pure culture of an organism is needed for the formation and harvesting of a pure product during and after growth in a fermenter vessel. The organism must be supplied with suitable conditions for growth and without competition for maximum efficiency.
- The vessel should be sterilised beforehand and an appropriate sterile medium used. During use the vessel openings must be protected from contamination by filters,and aseptic conditions and handling are required to maintain purity.
- Forced aeration may be needed, for maximum growth of aerobes, which may also mix the culture to improve contact with nutrients. Mixing may be improved by a separate mixer.
- Temperature monitoring and control are required to maintain constant conditions and water-jackets remove excess heat produced during the culture process.
- Commercially, sophisticated monitors are used to improve control of temperature and pH, and air inlets may use spargers or other devices to improve aeration.

❑ **Action**   Draw an annotated diagram of a batch culture fermenter.

Antibiotic production

- The fermenter is inoculated with a culture of *Penicillium notatum*, which then grows under the optimum conditions provided in the fermenter.
- It takes about 30 hours for penicillin production to begin. The penicillin is secreted by the fungus and accumulates in the medium. The delay in production occurs because penicillin is a **secondary metabolite**. It is produced **after** the exponential phase of growth is completed, when glucose is depleted.
- After about six days the culture fluid mixture is filtered and the penicillin is extracted and purified. That is, the culture medium, after filtering, is retained and processed.
  This type of fermentation is known as a batch culture. The fermenter has to be emptied, cleaned and sterilised, ready for the next batch.

Antibiotic production is a **secondary metabolism**, i.e. the antibiotic is produced at a period in the life of the fungus when there is a change away from its optimum conditions. This reflects the need for the organism, when free living, to reduce competition when food sources are depleted.

(Primary metabolism is the norm, when the fungus is metabolising glucose to release energy and increasing its own biomass. Continuous cultivation is suitable for products known as primary metabolites. This allows production to continue for much longer, as nutrients are added throughout the process and the products are continuously being removed. Many products including alcohol and insulin are produced in this way.)

4.5 Population growth

Humans are influenced by the same regulatory forces that determine population size in other organisms. However, humans are able to have a degree of control over their environment, leading to the modification of natural ecosystems. As the human population increases so does our effect on the environment.

Population growth in bacteria

A population is a group of organisms of a single species interbreeding. Humans inhabit almost all parts of the Earth; the human population is a global population. Populations of most species do not increase at the incredible rate that the human population is rising. Various factors keep them in check.

Consider a population of bacteria being cultured in a fermenter. If conditions of temperature and nutrients are favourable, the following phases of growth occur:

- The **lag phase** – this may last from a few minutes to several days. There is little cell multiplication or growth. (As only a few individuals are present initially the rate of growth is very slow.) This is a period of adaptation or preparation for growth, with intense metabolic activity, notably enzyme synthesis.
- The **exponential phase** – as numbers increase, providing there is no factor limiting growth, more individuals become available for reproduction. In the case of bacteria the cells begin to divide at a constant rate with the population doubling per unit time. The cell population increases geometrically. This rate of increase cannot be maintained indefinitely.
- The **stationary phase** – population growth enters this phase when the birth rate of new individuals is equal to the death rate of older ones. Certain factors limit the population growth. The population has reached its maximum size. This is known as the **carrying capacity** for the particular environment in which the population occurs. This describes the limit to the number of individuals that an area can support.
- The **death phase** – when death rate is greater than birth rate. This may occur when all the food in a nutrient solution has been used up.

- ❑ *Action* Draw a generalised graph of population growth (S-shaped curve) with the stages of growth as shown by a liquid culture of yeast or bacteria.
  Annotate the graph with the four phases described above.

The S-shaped curve is typical of any species colonising new habitats. There is a period of slow growth as the species adapts to the habitat, followed by a period of rapid growth with little environmental resistance. The graph then levels off as the population reaches its carrying capacity. If one factor becomes in short supply, then this can limit the growth of the population which then goes into decline.

Environmental resistance includes all the factors which keep numbers in check or 'limit the growth of a population' such as food availability, predation, parasitism, disease, overcrowding, competition and accumulation of toxic waste. Thus, population growth slows down due to environmental resistance. When humans first evolved the population would have been controlled in a similar way. Various factors in the environment kept the population stable with disease or food supply being the main factors. Nowadays, technology has made it possible for the human population to be maintained at much higher levels than the environment would have allowed in the past. These technological advances include improved methods of food production, medicines and disease control.

Human population growth

During the last 150 years the human population of the world has grown at an alarming rate. In 1850 the population was one billion, 80 years later it had doubled to two billion and by 1980 it had reached 4.5 billion. By the year 2000 it had reached 6.1 billion and it is estimated that it will reach 6.8 billion by 2010 and rise to 11 billion by 2050.

❑ **_Action_**   Draw a graph showing human population growth

Wherever humans live they change the natural environment. They cut down forests to grow crops and build roads and houses. Fossil fuels are burnt. Humans pollute the environment with pesticides, fertilisers, sewage and industrial waste. In some parts of the world wild animals are killed for food, with some species becoming endangered. Human impact is decreasing biodiversity.

Industrialisation in the developed regions of the world during the 19th century was eventually accompanied by a fall in the death rates, and later by a fall in the birth rates. In developing countries the situation is different. Social and health changes have reduced infant mortality in some areas but birth rate remains high, resulting in high rates of population growth.

Food production

There are still many parts of the world where food production is insufficient to support a rise in population. Many people are short of food and many die as a result of poor nutrition. Worldwide there is sufficient food to feed all the world's population. The problem is that this food is not where it needs to be. The UK produces enough food to feed the population and the food wasted would feed thousands more. The farmers of the European Union produce far more food than required, allowing food to be exported. With the help of agencies such as Oxfam some of this food is sent to parts of the world where populations are starving. This acts as a temporary measure to relieve the suffering of famine that may have been caused by lack of rainfall, flood or war.

Disease

Infectious disease can be a stabilising factor preventing population growth. Medical advances, such as the treatment of disease with antibiotics and limiting their spread with vaccines, have been very successful. Medical technology has also helped to reduce death rates from other diseases such as cancers and inherited diseases. In some parts of the world people are living longer than they would have done in the past so population numbers are increasing.

On the other hand, diseases such as HIV/AIDS have spread to all parts of the world, killing more than a million people each year. In addition the disease weakens an HIV positive individual's immune system making them susceptible to other diseases such as TB.

Annually, about eight million people contract TB. 80% of these people live in 22 countries. Two million of these die from TB. The World Health Organisation estimates that one third of new TB infections are in people with HIV/AIDS.

The AIDS pandemic has lowered the estimated world population level for the year 2050 from 11 billion to 9.5 billion. This is mainly caused by the massive toll of AIDS in Africa.

4.5 Recycling nutrients

Although ecosystems receive an inexhaustible influx of solar energy, chemical elements are available only in limited amounts. Life therefore depends on the recycling of essential chemical elements. Microorganisms play an important role in the process of decay, releasing compounds of these elements from the bodies of dead organisms.

Carbon cycle

Carbon dioxide is added to the air by the respiration of animals, plants and microorganisms and by the combustion of fossil fuels. Photosynthesis takes place on so great a scale that it re-uses on a daily basis almost as much carbon dioxide as is released into the atmosphere. This is the basis of the carbon cycle. The production of carbohydrates, proteins and fats contributes to plant growth and subsequently to animal growth through complex food webs. The dead remains of plants and animals are then acted upon by saprobionts in the soil which ultimately release gaseous CO_2 back to the atmosphere.
In past times large quantities of dead organisms accumulated in anaerobic conditions and so were prevented from decaying. In time they formed coal, oil and other fossil fuels. The burning of these fuels returns more CO_2 to the atmosphere and has resulted in a rise in CO_2 in the atmosphere, particularly over the last 50 years.

❑ **Action**   Draw a labelled diagram of the carbon cycle linking the processes of photosynthesis, respiration, decomposition, fossilisation and combustion.

Nitrogen cycle

The nitrogen cycle is the flow of organic and inorganic nitrogen within an ecosystem where there is an interchange between nitrogenous compounds and atmospheric nitrogen.

Living organisms need nitrogen to make amino acids, proteins and nucleic acids. Plants and animals are unable to use nitrogen gas. Instead plants take in nitrates in solution through their roots. The organic nitrogen compounds produced by plants are transferred through the food chain when consumers eat plants. When plants and animals die the minerals locked in their bodies, together with the excretory products of animals, must be decomposed in order to release the minerals back into the soil.
Bacteria are the key organisms involved in the process. The main processes involved are as follows:
- **Putrefaction** – bacteria, and fungi, decompose dead plants and animals, faeces and urine into ammonium ions. This process is also called ammonification.
- **Nitrification** – the ammonia formed in putrefaction is converted by nitrification via nitrites to nitrates. Various bacteria are involved. For example, ammonia is converted to nitrite by *Nitrosomonas* and nitrite to nitrate by *Nitrobacter*. These bacteria require aerobic conditions.
- **Nitrogen fixation** – atmospheric nitrogen can be converted directly into nitrogen compounds by nitrogen fixing bacteria. Free living nitrogen fixing bacteria include *Azotobacter.* These account for most of the nitrogen fixation. There are also symbiotic nitrogen fixing bacteria, *Rhizobium*, found in the root nodules of legumes (peas, beans and clover).
- **Denitrification** – nitrogen is lost from ecosystems by denitrification. This is a particular problem in waterlogged soils with anaerobic conditions where anaerobic bacteria, such as *Pseudomonas,* can reduce nitrates and ammonium ions back to nitrogen.

Human activities can improve the circulation of nitrogen.

- By fixing atmospheric nitrogen artificially using chemical processes that convert it to fertilizers.
- Large amount of animal waste from stock rearing is used as manure.
- Sewage disposal boosts organic nitrogen supplies.
- Microorganisms can be used for making compost and silage.
- Farming practices such as:
  - ✓ planting fields of clover to encourage nitrogen fixation.
  - ✓ draining land and reducing anaerobic conditions.
  - ✓ ploughing fields in order to improve aeration of the soil.
  - ✓

The last two activities ensure that anaerobic bacteria cannot compete with aerobic bacteria thus preventing denitrification.

❏ **Action**   Draw a labelled diagram to illustrate the processes of decay, nitrification, denitrification and nitrogen fixation.

4.6 Homeostasis

Homeostasis

The AS course covered information about enzymes and explained that they control chemical reactions in cells operating best within narrow limits of pH and temperature. Other internal factors, such as the composition of the tissue fluid that bathes the cells, have also to be kept as stable as possible.
Homeostasis means the maintenance of a constant environment within a living organism.
Examples of homeostatic control systems include; maintaining constant blood glucose levels, thermoregulation; osmoregulation function of the kidney.

The homeostatic process

- All homeostatic processes involve a **detector** (or sensor) which detects a stimulus. A stimulus is a change in the level of the factor being controlled. That is, a detector monitors the factor being controlled.
- When the detector senses a change from the normal, it informs a **coordinator,** which receives and controls information from the receptor. That is, the coordinator triggers an appropriate method of correcting the deviation.
- The coordinator communicates with one or more **effectors** which carry out the corrective procedures.
- Once the correction is made and the factor returned to normal, information is fed back to the detector which then 'switches off'.
- This is what happens in most biological control systems, i.e. the coordinator is no longer alerted to the deviation from the normal. This is called a **negative feedback**.

❏ *Action*   Construct a flowchart to illustrate the homeostatic process.

4.6 Control systems regulate life

Many metabolic reactions taking place in living organisms produce waste products which can be toxic if allowed to accumulate. Excretion is the removal from the body of waste products of metabolism. (*This should not be confused with 'egestion' which is the removal of waste material that has passed through the body unchanged.*) In humans the waste products include carbon dioxide, urea and bile.

The kidney

The kidney has two main functions:
- Removal of nitrogenous metabolic waste from the body.
- Osmoregulation, the mechanism by which the balance of water and dissolved solutes is regulated.

The production of urea

Urea is a poisonous chemical made by the liver. If there is too much protein in the diet any excess has to be broken down (as it cannot be stored like carbohydrates and fats). The amino acids, which make up protein, are **deaminated** in the liver. The reaction produces ammonia, which is quickly converted to urea. Urea is released into the blood, and travels around the body until it is removed by the kidneys.

Structure of the kidney

❑ *Action*   1. Draw a labelled diagram of the mammalian urinary system.
              Label - renal artery, renal vein, kidney, ureter, bladder, urethra.
              2. Draw a section through a kidney (L.S.)
              Label – cortex, medulla, pelvis; include the position of a nephron.

Humans have two kidneys and these are the main organs that filter waste products from the blood. Each kidney is made up of about a million **nephrons**. Each nephron is made up of four functional parts a **Bowman's capsule**, a **proximal tubule**, the **loop of Henle** and a **distal tubule** leading to a **collecting duct**.

Within each Bowman's capsule is a knot of blood capillaries known as the **glomerulus.** The blood supply to the nephron begins as an afferent arteriole serving the glomerulus. From the glomerulus the blood is carried by the efferent arteriole to two other capillary structures:
- a capillary network serving the proximal and distal convoluted tubules.
- a capillary network running beside the loop of Henle and known as the **vasa recta**.

❑ *Action*   Draw a single nephron.
              Label - afferent arteriole, efferent arteriole, glomerulus, Bowman's capsule,
              proximal convoluted tubule, loop of Henle, distal convoluted tubule, collecting duct.

Functioning of the kidney

The functioning of the nephron involves three different processes
- ultra filtration
- selective reabsorption
- secretion.

The osmoregulatory function of the kidney is controlled by hormones.

Ultra filtration

- Ultrafiltration is a filtration under pressure that separates small soluble molecules from the blood plasma. It is the process by which small molecules such as water, glucose, urea and salts are filtered from the knot of capillaries, the glomerulus, into the Bowman's capsule.

- The blood entering the glomerulus is separated from the space inside the Bowman's capsule by two cell layers and a basement membrane.

- **Action**   Draw a diagram of the detailed structure of the site of ultrafiltration (include basement membrane, endothelial cells of blood capillary, podocytes).

- The structure of the glomerulus and capsule allows ultrafiltration to take place. The basement membrane of the capillary forms the selective barrier between the blood and the nephron and it acts as a molecular sieve.
  - ✓ The first cell layer is the wall of the capillary. This single layer of cells contains many small gaps.
  - ✓ The basement membrane between the two cell layers acts as a filter during ultrafiltration.
  - ✓ The second cell layer makes up the wall of the Bowman's capsule. The epithelial cells in this layer are called podocytes.
- The sieve action allows smaller-sized molecules to pass through but retains in the capillaries the blood proteins and cells.
- Most of the pressure producing the filtration comes from the hydrostatic pressure of the blood in the glomerular capillaries. This pressure is amplified by the pressure in the capsule produced by the narrow efferent vessels and also by the water potential in the blood produced by the colloidal plasma proteins. The glomerular pressure can be altered by changes in the diameter of the afferent and efferent arterioles entering and leaving the glomerulus.

Selective reabsorption

Selective reabsorption is the process by which useful products such as glucose and salts are reabsorbed back into the blood as the filtrate flows along the nephron.
- All the glucose and most of the water and salt (sodium and chloride ions) are reabsorbed in the proximal convoluted tubule. Small amounts of water and salt are reabsorbed in the distal tubule. Most of the remaining water is reabsorbed in the collecting duct by a mechanism which involves the loop of Henle.
- Reabsorption of glucose and salts takes place by active transport. Water is reabsorbed passively by osmosis following the transport of salt.
- The loops of Henle collectively concentrate salts in the tissue fluid of the medulla of the kidney.
- The high concentration of salt then causes an osmotic flow of water out of the collecting ducts thereby concentrating the urine and making it hypertonic to the blood.
- The loop of Henle uses the principle of a **hair-pin counter current multiplier.**
- As fluid flows up the ascending limb, Na^+ and Cl^- is actively pumped out of the ascending limb into the tissue fluid of the surrounding medulla where a low water potential is created. The ascending limb is relatively impermeable to water while the descending limb is permeable. Water leaves the filtrate of the descending limb by osmosis and is carried away by the blood in the vasa recta.
- The content of the descending limb become progressively more concentrated and reaches its maximum concentration at the tip of the loop; as it flows up the ascending limb the fluid becomes more and more dilute. Since the surrounding fluid also becomes more concentrated an osmotic gradient is maintained down to the tip of the loop. The effect at one level is slight but the overall effect is multiplied by the length of the hair-pin. The result is that a region of particularly high salt concentration is produced in a deep part of the medulla, resulting in the osmotic extraction of water from the adjacent permeable collecting ducts.

The cells in the wall of the proximal convoluted tubule are adapted by having:
- microvilli providing a large surface area for absorption.
- numerous mitochondria providing ATP for active transport.

- **Action**   Draw detail of cells from the wall of the proximal convoluted tubule.

Osmoregulation

Osmoregulation is the homeostatic control of body water.

Mammals have to maintain a balance between water gain and water loss. Humans gain most of their water from drinking and from food. Most of the water is lost as urine. Other losses are due to sweating, keeping exchange surfaces moist, and loss in faeces.

Osmoregulation operates on the principle of negative feedback, typical of homeostasis.

- ✓ The **receptors** responsible for detecting changes are located in the **hypothalamus**, at the base of the brain.
- ✓ The posterior lobe of **pituitary** acts as the **coordinator.**
- ✓ The **collecting ducts** of kidney act as the **effector.**

- The permeability of the walls of the collecting duct, like the walls of the distal convoluted tubule, is subject to hormonal control. This hormonal effect, together with the hypertonic interstitial fluids built up by the loop of Henle in the medulla, determine whether hypotonic or hypertonic urine is released from the kidney.
- ADH makes the walls of the collecting duct permeable so that water is reabsorbed and the urine has a concentration close to the concentration of the tissues near the bottom of the loop, that is, hypertonic to the general body fluids.
- The amount of water reabsorbed is controlled by a **feedback system**. Negative feedback restores the normal osmotic concentration if blood is diluted or becomes more concentrated.
- A fall in water potential of the blood may be caused by one or a combination of factors – reduced water intake, sweating, intake of large amounts of salt. The concentration of sodium chloride in the blood is an indirect indication of the volume of water in the body. The hypothalamus is sensitive to the concentration of sodium chloride in the blood flowing through it. If the water content is low a fall in water potential is detected by **osmoreceptors** (osmotic receptors) in the hypothalamus and results in nerve impulses passing to the posterior pituitary gland which then releases **ADH** into the blood stream. This has the following effects:
- ADH increases the permeability of the distal convoluted tubule and the collecting duct to water.
- This allows more water to be reabsorbed from these tubules into the region of high solute concentration in the medulla.
- More water is reabsorbed into the blood.
- Consequently the small volume of urine eventually eliminated is relatively concentrated.

☐ *Action*   What happens if a person drinks a lot of water?
           Describe how negative feedback restores the normal concentration if the water potential of the blood rises, that is, becomes less negative.

Kidney failure

When the kidneys are damaged by injury or disease the salt and water balance of body fluids is affected and wastes accumulate in the blood. In severe cases the function of the kidney needs to be taken over by the process of dialysis. This treatment will be necessary perhaps for the rest of the patient's life, or until the kidneys recover, or until a kidney transplant is available.

Diagnosis

Chronic kidney failure is usually characterised by the production of more urine than normal. ('Chronic' means a long-term condition.) A person with acute kidney failure will be feeling very ill. The failure of the kidneys to extract and excrete unwanted substances from the blood means that the contents of the blood and urine will be abnormal. Blood and urine tests may show unusual concentrations of various ions and molecules and the urine may even contain blood. Ultrasound tests may be used to detect any obstructions (such as kidney stones) that are preventing urine leaving the kidneys or flowing down the ureters.

Kidney dialysis

In severe cases the function of the kidneys needs to be taken over by the process of dialysis. There are two methods of kidney dialysis:

- Haemodialysis – where the patient's blood is passed through an artificial kidney machine, either in hospital or at home. Each session lasts between two to six hours and patients may need two or three sessions a week. Blood from the patient's vein is passed into the machine and back to the patient. In the machine blood passes through very small tubes made from a partially permeable membrane. On the other side of the membrane dialysis fluid flows along in the opposite direction. The dialysis fluid has the same water potential and concentration of ions and glucose that the patient's blood should have if their kidneys were working correctly. As a result, wastes, toxic molecules and excess fluid diffuse through the membrane into the dialysis fluid. Blood cells and protein molecules are too large to pass through the membrane so they remain in the blood. The 'purified' blood is returned to the patient and the dialysis fluid is discarded.

❑   *Action*   Draw and label a haemodialysis set-up.

- Peritoneal dialysis – this process is usually carried out in the home and is used more commonly than haemodialysis.
  The peritoneum is a layer of tissue that lines the cavity of the abdomen. It acts as a natural filter. The abdominal cavity contains fluid which bathes the internal organs. The method involves inserting a catheter into the abdominal cavity and dialysis fluid passes through the tube filling the cavity. The dialysis fluid is left there for some time allowing exchange between the blood and the fluid. The fluid is then drained off. It takes 30 to 45 minutes for the fluid to be introduced into the abdomen and the whole process takes several hours. During this time the patient can carry on with normal activities although they do need to have the fluid introduced and removed several times a day.

Advantages and disadvantages of the two types of dialysis

Haemodialysis	Peritoneal dialysis
More efficient	Less efficient
Takes several hours	Less time consuming
Patient connected to machine	Can carry on with normal activities
Expensive and in short supply	Inexpensive
Patient may experience fluctuations in blood volume or content	No large swings in blood volume or content
Less risk of infection	Greater risk of infection

Kidney transplants

Kidney transplants are by far the best treatment and nowadays transplant surgery is almost taken for granted. Many people owe their lives to a kidney transplant. However, a shortage of donors and the difficulty in making a tissue match means that people in need of a kidney often have to wait many years before a suitable kidney becomes available.

A person can survive perfectly well with one kidney so only one functional kidney is needed to restore the health of the patient. To prevent the recipient's immune system rejecting the kidney, the tissue type and blood group of recipient and donor must be a close match. The general success rate for kidney transplantation is around 80%. This can be even higher when the donor is a close relative because there is a good chance of a close tissue match. If the kidney is rejected then the patient must return to dialysis before another operation is attempted. Normally, the patient takes immunosuppressant drugs to reduce the risk of rejection.

Ethical issues

In the UK alone about 2,000 kidney transplant operations are carried out each year. However, there are about twice as many people on the waiting list for a suitable donor.
The operation has a good chance of success as long as the transplant is completed within 48 hours of the removal of the donor kidney. Most kidneys come from people who have consented to the medical use of their organs after death and who carry a donor card. However there is a shortage of such donors as not many people carry donor cards.

On a world-wide scale there is a huge demand for donors. The fact that the donor can manage with only one kidney has fuelled the growth of a global trade in human kidneys. International rings have been uncovered where people living in poverty are persuaded to sell kidneys to a middle-man who then makes a considerable profit on the deal when he sells the kidney on to a recipient. This raises a number of ethical issues. The donors run a greater risk of illness if their remaining kidney fails or if the operation to remove the donated kidney is performed badly. These people are being exploited.

It may be possible to genetically engineer animals of other species so that their cells do not carry antigens that our immune system would attack. This is being researched in pigs. However, there are major ethical issues associated with this, and many religious groups and individuals find this type of treatment unacceptable.

4.7 Nervous System

For the nervous system to carry out its function effectively it is dependent upon a continuous input of information from inside the body and from the environment. This input is detected by sensory receptors and relayed to effectors. That is, responses to all stimuli involve the reception of information and its transfer from the receptor to an effector via the nervous system.

The mammalian nervous system is dual in nature. The central nervous system (CNS) co-ordinates and controls the activities of the animal. The peripheral nervous system, the nerves and ganglia, forms the connecting link between the organs and the CNS. Many body functions and actions are controlled by reflex actions which involve both parts of the nervous system.

The nervous system

The nervous system:
- Detects changes or stimuli inside the body and from the surroundings.
- Processes the information.
- Initiates responses.

Receptors which range from specialised sensory cells, such as those in the skin, to the more complex sense organs such as the ear and eye, **detect** the information from inside the body and from the surroundings.

It is the role of the **central nervous system (CNS)**, which is made up of the brain and spinal cord, to process the information and initiate a response.

Effectors bring about **responses**. Effectors may be muscles or glands.

Sensory receptors detect one form of energy and convert it into electrical energy. They are acting as **transducers**. The electrical impulses travel along nerves and are called nerve impulses.

Some nerves bring information to the CNS and others take the information away.

There are a number of different types of receptors including thermoreceptors, which detect changes in temperature, photoreceptors which detect light, and chemoreceptors which detect chemicals.

Spinal cord

This is the part of the central nervous system that passes through and is protected by the vertebral column and from which most of the **peripheral nerves** originate. It consists of a central area of grey matter, made up mainly of nerve cell bodies. It is surrounded by an area of white matter made up of nerve fibres. Sensory fibres of the peripheral system enter the cord via the dorsal routes. The cell bodies of the sensory fibres are found in the dorsal root ganglia which lie alongside the spinal cord. The motor fibres leave via the ventral routes.

❑ *Action*   Draw a labelled diagram of a section through the spinal cord.
(Labels - central canal, grey matter, white matter, dorsal root, ventral root, sensory neurone, dorsal root ganglion, connector neurone, motor neurone, effector, meninges.)

The functions of the spinal cord are to relay impulses in and out of any particular point along the cord, and to relay impulses up and down the body, including to and from the brain.

Reflex arc

- A reflex action is a rapid, involuntary response resulting from nervous impulses initiated by a stimulus. The action is involuntary in that the brain is not involved. Reflex actions are generally protective in function.
- The following describes a typical reflex action – the nerve pathways involved in the flexion of the arm in response to touching a hot surface.
- ✓ Stimulus – the hot surface.
- ✓ Receptor – temperature and pain receptors in the skin.
- ✓ Sensory neurone sends impulse to spinal cord.
- ✓ Relay neurone connects sensory neurone to motor neurone.
- ✓ Motor neurone sends impulse to an effector (muscle).
- ✓ Response – arm muscles contract and the hand is removed from surface.

❏ *Action*   Draw an annotated diagram of the nervous pathways of this reflex arc.

Although many reflexes are protective, actions such as blinking, coughing and swallowing are also coordinated by reflexes.

With any reflex action there is also a pathway for impulses to be sent to the brain via ascending nerve fibres that originate at synapses in the grey matter of the spinal cord. The brain may store this information or it may relate the information with sense data from, say, the eyes. As a result of receiving this extra information impulses may be sent from the brain to modify the response. Sometimes the response is over-ridden by the brain along inhibitory nerve fibres.

4.7 Neurones

Structure of neurones

Neurones are highly specialised cells that generate and transmit nerve impulses.
There are three types of **neurones**:
- **Sensory** – which bring impulses from the sense organs or receptors into the CNS.
- **Motor** – these carry impulses from the CNS to the effector organs (muscles or glands).
- **Connector** (Intermediate or relay) – these receive impulses from sensory neurones or other intermediate neurones and relay them to motor neurones or other intermediate neurones.

❑ *Action*   1. Draw and label a mammalian **motor** neurone.
(Labels - dendrites, cell body, nucleus, axon, myelin sheath, Schwann cell, nodes of Ranvier, nerve/axon endings).
2. Describe the functions of the parts labelled.

Each cell consists of a cell body containing a nucleus and granular cytoplasm containing many ribosomes. These ribosomes are grouped together forming Nissl granules which are concerned with the formation of neurotransmitter substances. Many thin extensions carry impulses towards the cell body. The short extensions are called **dendrites**. These receive impulses from other nerve cells and carry the information towards the cell body. Some neurones also have a long membrane-covered cytoplasmic extension, the **axon**, which transmits impulses from the cell body. At its end, an axon divides into branches which form **synapses** with other neurones.
Peripheral neurones are surrounded by and supported by **Schwann cells**. In some cases these grow around the axons of the nerve cells to form a multilayered fatty **myelin sheath** found only in vertebrate nervous systems. This acts as an electrical insulator and speeds up the transmission of impulses. The myelin sheath has thin areas at intervals, **nodes of Ranvier**, which are important in impulse transmission.

The nerve impulse

The electrical change associated with a typical nerve impulse is very small (50 millivolts). Nevertheless, nerve impulses can be recorded and measured using an apparatus which is sensitive to small electrical changes. Impulses can be picked up from the nerve through a pair of microelectrodes and fed into a **cathode ray oscilloscope.** This can measure the magnitude and speed of transmission of impulses and analyse the pattern of impulses generated in different parts of the nervous system.

Transmission of nerve impulses

Neurones transmit electrical impulses along the cell surface membrane surrounding the axon. Experiments involving inserting microelectrodes into axons and measuring the changes in electrical charge have shown that in a resting axon, the inside of the membrane has a negative electrical charge compared to the outside.
- ✓ This **resting potential** is the potential difference between the inside and the outside of a membrane when a nerve impulse is not being conducted.
- ✓ Resting potentials are typically minus values, the minus indicating the inside is negative with respect to the outside. The membrane is said to be polarised. How does this happen?
- ✓ Sodium and potassium ions are transported across the membrane against a concentration gradient by active transport.
- ✓ This involves sodium-potassium exchange pumps (these are trans-membrane proteins) which maintain the concentration and an uneven distribution of sodium ions and potassium ions across the membrane.

- However, the Na$^+$ ions are passed out faster than the K$^+$ ions are brought in. Also K$^+$ ions are able to diffuse back out faster than the Na$^+$ ions can diffuse back in. The net result is that the outside of the membrane is positive compared to the inside.
- The outward movement of positive ions means that the inside becomes slightly negative.

The action potential

When a nerve impulse is initiated the resting potential changes.

Nerve impulses are due to changes in the permeability of nerve cell membrane to K$^+$ ions and Na$^+$ ions which leads to changes in the potential difference across the membrane and the formation of action potential.

- Suitable stimulation of an axon results in change of potential across the membrane from a negative inside value of about –70mV to a positive inside value of +40mV. This change is called an **action potential** and lasts about three milliseconds. The membrane is said to be **depolarised**.
- When the resting potential is re-established, the axon membrane is said to be repolarised.
- The action potential is the result of a sudden increase in the permeability of the membrane to Na$^+$. This allows a sudden influx of Na$^+$ which depolarises the membrane.
- A fraction of a second after this depolarisation the K$^+$ diffuse out and repolarises the membrane. There is an overshoot of K$^+$ leaving as the K$^+$/Na$^+$ pump restores the ionic balance. This is called the **refractory period** during which another action potential cannot be generated. This time delay ensures a unidirectional impulse and limits frequency.

❑ **Action** Draw and interpret an oscilloscope trace (showing an action and resting potential).

How the action potential travels along an axon.

The action potential causes a small electric current across the membrane and as a portion of the membrane is depolarised, depolarisation of the next portion is initiated. There is a series of local currents propagated along the axon. The sodium pump is active all the time and behind the transmission; this pump restores the resting potential. Once the resting potential is restored, another impulse can be transmitted. As the impulse progresses the out-flux of K$^+$ causes the neurone to be repolarised behind the impulse.

Synapses

Neurones are not in direct contact with each other but are separated by tiny gaps known as synapses. The main role of the synapse is to convey action potentials between neurones. A range of drugs function by interfering with the neurotransmitters involved in synaptic transmission.

Structure of a synapse

Most junctions between neurones take the form of chemical synapses. Branches of axons lie close to dendrites of other neurones but do not touch; there is a gap of about 20um between them. When impulses are transmitted, this gap is crossed by the secretion of a neurotransmitter from the axon membrane (pre-synaptic membrane), which diffuses across the space to stimulate the dendritic membrane (post-synaptic membrane).

❑ **Action**   1. Draw a diagram of a synapse.
(Label - synaptic knob, synaptic vesicle, mitochondria, pre-synaptic membrane, synaptic cleft, post-synaptic membrane.)

Synaptic transmission

The arrival of the impulses at the **synaptic knob** alters its permeability allowing **calcium ions** to enter. The influx of calcium ions causes the **synaptic vesicle** to fuse with the **pre-synaptic membrane** so releasing the **transmitter** (acetylcholine) into the **synaptic cleft**. When the transmitter diffuses across the gap (synaptic cleft), it attaches to a receptor site on the **post-synaptic membrane**, depolarising it and so initiating an impulse in the next neurone.
The postsynaptic membrane contains specific protein receptors with which the transmitter molecules combine. Once combined, protein channels open up in the membrane, allowing sodium ions to diffuse from the cleft into the postsynaptic neurone. If the membrane becomes sufficiently depolarised, an action potential is initiated in the axon of the postsynaptic neurone.
Acetylcholine, when released, is quickly destroyed by enzymes in the synaptic cleft, so its effect is limited and the merging of impulses is prevented. If insufficient acetylcholine is released, the post-synaptic membrane will not be stimulated. The enzyme which destroys acetylcholine is called **cholinesterase.** The resulting choline and ethanoic acid diffuse back across the synaptic cleft to reform acetylcholine. ATP is required to re-form transmitter molecules and store them in vesicles.

Another transmitter substance is **noradrenaline**.
It occurs, together with acetylcholine, in the involuntary nervous system.

❑ **Action**   Draw annotated diagrams to illustrate synaptic transmission.

Functions of synapses

The function of the synapse is to convey action potentials between neurones.
• Transmit information between neurones.
• Pass impulses in one direction only.
• Act as junctions – since synaptic vesicles are present only in the knob of the presynaptic neurone, impulses can only pass across a synapse in one direction.
• Filter out low level stimuli. That is, remove 'background noise' from the nervous system.
• To protect the response system from overstimulation.

Effects of drugs

A **psychoactive drug** is a chemical substance that acts primarily on the central nervous system where it alters brain function resulting in temporary changes in perception, mood, consciousness and behaviour. Most of these drugs were originally developed to be used therapeutically as medication. Because psychoactive substances bring about subjective changes in consciousness and mood which the user may find pleasant (e.g. euphoria) or advantageous (e.g. increased alertness), many psychoactive substances are abused, that is, used outside of the guidance of a medical professional and for reasons other than their original purpose. With sustained use physical dependence may develop, making the cycle of abuse even more difficult to interrupt. Examples of psychoactive drugs include tobacco, cannabis, amphetamines, ecstasy, cocaine, heroin etc.

Most drugs that affect the nervous system influence the transmission of nerve impulses across synapses. These drugs can be classified into two types:
- ✓ Excitory drugs, which amplify the process of synaptic transmission.
- ✓ Inhibitory drugs, such as Beta-blockers, mainly used to treat heart disease, modify the effects that the neurotransmitters have on the post-synaptic membrane.

Amplification at the synapse may be due to chemicals mimicking the action of natural transmitters. That is, they have the same shape and affect the post-synaptic neurone in the same way that the transmitter would. They may prevent the breakdown of the transmitter, for example, by inhibiting the enzyme that normally does this.

- Organophosphorous insecticides, block the enzyme that breaks down the transmitter substance once they are attached to the receptor proteins of the post-synaptic membrane. This prolongs the effect of the neurotransmitters. Without cholinesterase, acting as a cholinesterase inhibitor, acetylcholine remains in the synaptic cleft and causes repeated firing of the postsynaptic neurone. If the inhibitor is acting at a neuromuscular junction, repeated contractions of the muscle occurs. That is, the nervous system becomes overactive and muscles contract uncontrollably.

- Drugs like amphetamines ('speed') (originally prescribed to treat obesity) and its related drug, ecstasy, are excitory drugs that stimulate the release of neurotransmitters such as noradrenaline. Chemicals such as caffeine and nicotine also reduce the threshold for excitation of the post-synaptic membranes.

If a drug is taken over a period of time then the synapse may be modified to adjust to its use. For example, if the drug blocks particular receptors at synapses, then new receptors may be made to make up for the ones that are no longer in use. This means that more drug has to be taken to have the same effect. This is known as tolerance to the drug. An increasing tolerance indicates an increase in dependency on the drug. Dependency occurs when, as a result of changes to the CNS, the individual can no longer manage without the drug. A distinction may be made between physical dependency and psychological dependency.

- ✓ Physical dependency occurs because there have been changes in the structure and the way the neurones of the brain work. If the individual stops taking the drug they suffer from withdrawal symptoms. Withdrawal from heroin produces some of the worst withdrawal symptoms.
- ✓ Psychological dependency is due to what is happening in the brain as a result of taking the drug. The individual does not experience withdrawal symptoms but constantly craves the drug, in a similar way in which a person feels when they are very hungry or thirsty.

Alcohol is an example of a drug to which both physical and psychological dependency may develop. It also affects neurotransmitters in the brain. It is a depressant and if drunk in large amounts can kill. Inhibition of various areas of the brain causes drowsiness and eventually unconsciousness. It can cause coma. Regular high consumption over many years may damage the liver, causing cirrhosis. This condition normally results in death.

Nervous diseases

Motor neurone disease (MND)

MND is a rare condition caused by the degeneration of the motor nerve cells in the spinal cord and brain that control the voluntary muscles. MND gets worse over time. Parts of the brain dealing with intelligence and awareness are not affected. There is no cure and life expectancy will be affected depending on how symptoms progress. Most people who have MND will die from it within five years but there are some exceptions.

MND develops at different speeds in different individuals and affects people in different ways.
The disease usually begins very gradually and the sufferer may just feel tired.
Other symptoms may develop:
- ✓ Gradual impairment of the use of arms and legs.
- ✓ Muscle twitch and pain and stiffness around any joint where the muscles are affected.
- ✓ The throat muscles may be involved and this may lead to difficulties in swallowing and speech.
- ✓ The chest muscles may be affected leading to breathing difficulties.

Diagnosis of the disease is difficult. Often an electromyography is used in which a needle is inserted into various muscles to measure electrical activity.
The cause of MND is unknown and there is no known treatment to halt or reverse its progression.
The drug riluzole has been shown to slow down the progress of the disease but with an average gain in life expectancy of only two months. Drugs can ease some of the symptoms. According to the MND Association a number of complementary therapies, including acupuncture, aromatherapy and homeopathy, may help. Physiotherapy can help to maximise mobility.

Research is being carried out into possible new treatments. In the future scientists hope to use stem cells to treat the condition.

Parkinson's disease

The Parkinson's Disease Society estimates that there are about 120,000 people in the UK with the disease - that's one in 500 of the general population - and approximately 10,000 people are diagnosed each year.

Parkinson's is a progressive neurological condition that is usually diagnosed after the age of 60, although 5% of sufferers diagnosed will be under 40 at the time of diagnosis.

It is a slow, progressive disease caused by the death of brain cells that produce dopamine. This chemical is an important neurotransmitter (a chemical that carries signals between the neurons in the brain) which enables an individual to perform smooth, coordinated movements. A person with Parkinson's will develop symptoms once 80 per cent of these cells are dead.

At first a person may notice tremor in their arms or legs and this gradually becomes greater. With time the individual finds movement increasingly difficult to control. After several years people with the disease may develop a shuffling walk without arm movement. Because Parkinson's disease attacks the part of the brain that controls our movements it affects activities we take for granted, such as talking, walking, swallowing and writing. Symptoms include repetitive shaking, slowness of movement and muscle stiffness.

There's no cure but a lot can be done to relieve symptoms, especially in the early stages. The aim is to replace the missing dopamine in the brain. This can be carried out very effectively with a drug called levodopa - a synthetic chemical that is converted into dopamine in the brain. However, there can be severe side-effects with prolonged usage.

Occupational therapists and physiotherapists help people manage their condition by assisting with movement and providing advice on how to maintain independence in everyday life. Speech and language therapists help with communication or swallowing difficulties.

Stroke

In the UK every year an estimated 150,000 people suffer a stroke, that's one person every five minutes! It is the third most common form of death in the UK .About 80% of strokes are due to a blood clot forming in a blood vessel supplying blood to the brain. Then part of the brain becomes starved of oxygen and the neurones in that area die. This can result in a loss of function or sensation associated with the part of the brain that is affected. For example, a stroke in the right side of the brain (cerebrum) is likely to affect movement on the left side of the body. A stroke on the left side of the brain will affect language. Memory is often impaired no matter which side of the brain the stroke affects.

Common symptoms include:

- numbness, weakness or paralysis on one side of the body (signs of this may be a drooping arm, leg or lower eyelid, or a dribbling mouth)

- slurred speech or difficulty finding words or understanding speech

- sudden blurred vision or loss of sight

- confusion or unsteadiness

- a severe headache.

Immediate treatment for a stroke may include clot-bursting drugs such as streptokinase, if the stroke is the result of a blood clot in the brain. This must be administered no later than six hours after the onset of the stroke if it is to be effective. Taking aspirin regularly in the days following the stroke can reduce the recurrence.
As soon as possible the patient undergoes rehabilitation therapy. This aims to help patients relearn skills that have been lost when their brain was damaged.

The risk factors for strokes are the same as those for coronary heart disease. An individual with high blood pressure (hypertension) has a considerably increased risk of having a stroke. Smoking causes increase blood pressure and so makes the chance of a stroke more likely.

5.1 Replication and protein synthesis

DNA is a molecule which carries instructions, or a blueprint, for the construction and behaviour of cells and the way in which they grow together to form a complete living organism. DNA also has the ability to make perfect copies of itself, over and over again. DNA has two major functions in the cell:
- **Replication**, in dividing cells.
- Carrying information for **protein synthesis** in all cells.

Replication

Chromosomes must make copies of themselves so that when cells divide, each daughter cell must receive an exact copy of the genetic information. This copying of DNA is called replication and takes place in a cell during interphase. Replication occurs as follows:
- The hydrogen bonds holding the base pairs together break and the two halves of the molecule separate.
- **DNA unwinds** and as the strands separate **DNA polymerase** catalyses the addition of free nucleotides to the exposed bases.
- Each chain acts as a **template** so that free nucleotides can be joined to their **complementary bases** by the enzyme, DNA polymerase.
- The result is two DNA molecules, each made up of one newly synthesised chain and one chain that has been conserved from the original molecule.
- This is called the **semi-conservative hypothesis.** This theory was proposed by Watson and Crick in 1954 and confirmed shortly after by the evidence provided by Meselson and Stahl's experiments.

The experiments involved the use of an ultra-centrifuge. This rotates centrifuge tubes containing liquid suspensions at very high speeds which results in the denser particles separating out at a lower point in the tube than the lighter particles.

1. The scientists cultured the bacterium, *Escherichia coli,* for several generations on a medium containing amino acids made with the heavy isotope of nitrogen ^{15}N. The bacteria incorporated the ^{15}N into their nucleotides and then into their DNA so that all the DNA contained ^{15}N. They extracted the bacterial DNA and centrifuged it. The DNA settled at a low point in the tube.
2. The ^{15}N bacteria were washed, then transferred to a medium containing the normal, lighter form of nitrogen, ^{14}N, and were allowed to divide once more.
3. When extracts of DNA from this first generation culture were centrifuged it was shown to have a mid point density since half the strand was made up of the original strand of ^{15}N DNA and the other half was made up of the new strand containing ^{14}N.
4. When extracts were taken from the second generation grown in ^{14}N the DNA settled at mid points and high points in the tube. This was conclusive evidence for the semi-conservative hypothesis.

❏ *Action*   1. Using coloured pens draw a diagram to show how two complementary strands of DNA unwind into separate strands. Starting with the parent strands carry out the process for three generations.

5.1 Protein synthesis

DNA also acts as a store of genetic information. Chromosomes are divided up into thousands of shorter sections called genes. The length of DNA making up a particular gene carries the information needed to make a particular protein. This information is called the genetic code. The codes carried by DNA determine what reactions can take place in an organism. Genes control the formation of enzymes which are proteins. By determining which enzymes are produced the DNA can determine the characteristics of an organism.

Nature of the genetic code

DNA is the starting point for protein synthesis since the sequence of bases on DNA, the genetic code, determines the primary structure of a protein, that is, the sequence by which various amino acids are joined together to form a particular polypeptide chain.

Why is the code a triplet code?
There are four different bases in DNA but there are over twenty different amino acids.
If one base coded for one amino acid it would be possible to make only four amino acids.
If two bases coded for one amino acid it would be possible to produce 16 different codes to make 16 amino acids.
Having three bases for each amino acid would give a permutation of 64 codes, more than enough to make 20 amino acids.
Amino acids are in fact coded by more than one DNA base triplet. Also there are some codes that do not code for amino acids at all! These have been called 'stop' and 'start' codes.

- It is the sequence of bases in the DNA chain that codes for the sequence of amino acids in a polypeptide.
- The portion of DNA which codes for a whole polypeptide is called a **gene**.
  (This is the basis of the one gene - one polypeptide hypothesis.)
- Each amino acid is coded for by three bases (the triplet code) called a **codon**.
- All the codons are **universal**, that is, they are exactly the same for all living organisms.
- The code is **non-overlapping** in that each triplet is read separately.

Protein synthesis

At AS you learnt that there are three different types of RNA, messenger RNA, ribosomal RNA and transfer RNA.
There are two main processes involved in making a protein:
- transcription – the formation of messenger RNA.
- translation – the translation of the code.

DNA, which does not leave the nucleus, acts as a template or blueprint for the production of mRNA, which carries the instructions needed for protein synthesis from the nucleus to the cytoplasm. The function of the ribosomes is to provide a suitable surface for the attachment of mRNA and the assembly of protein.

The process of protein synthesis occurs as follows:
Transcription
- The mRNA is copied from a specific region of DNA called the cistron.
- Often this is equivalent to a gene and codes for a specific polypeptide.

- The enzyme **RNA polymerase** links to the DNA at the beginning of the sequence to be copied. The double-stranded DNA first unwinds and then unzips in the relevant region. Only one of the DNA strands acts as a template against which a matching mRNA can be formed.
- Transcription occurs when free RNA nucleotides then align themselves opposite one of the two strands. Because of the complementary relationship between the bases in DNA and the free nucleotides, cytosine in the DNA attracts a guanine, guanine a cytosine, thymine an adenine, and adenine a uracil.
- **RNA polymerase** moves along the DNA forming bonds that add nucleotides one at a time to the RNA. This results in the synthesis of a molecule of mRNA alongside the unzipped portion of DNA. Behind the RNA polymerase the DNA strands rejoin to reform the double helix.
- Each amino acid was coded for by a DNA codon. The mRNA molecule carries complementary RNA codons.
- The mRNA carries the DNA code out of the nucleus through a nuclear pore to the cytoplasm and attaches itself to a ribosome consisting of ribosomal RNA and protein.

Translation

Amino acids are carried to the ribosomes by transfer RNA molecules (tRNA). Each tRNA carries its own specific amino acid at the amino acid attachment site. The specific amino acid is determined by the triplet of bases referred to as the anticodon. As there are over 20 amino acids there is the same number of different tRNA molecules. Energy from ATP is required for the specific amino acid to attach itself to the tRNA. This process is referred to as **activation.** Each ribosome is made up of two sub-units, with a smaller sub-unit having two sites for the attachment of tRNA molecules. This means that two tRNA molecules are associated with a ribosome at any one time.

The process of translation begins when the mRNA molecule attaches itself to the ribosome. The ribosome acts as a framework moving along the mRNA, reading the code, holding the **codon-anticodon complex** together until two amino acids join. The ribosome moves along adding one amino acid at a time until the polypeptide chain is assembled.
It happens like this:
- the first tRNA with the anticodon complementary to the first codon on the mRNA attaches itself to the ribosome. Then a second tRNA with an anticodon complementary to the second codon on the mRNA attaches to the other attachment site. The two amino acids are sufficiently close for a peptide bond to form between them. The first tRNA leaves the ribosome leaving an attachment site vacant. The ribosome now moves one codon along the mRNA strand.
- One site binds tRNA with the growing polypeptide; the other site is for tRNA carrying the next amino acid in the sequence.
- Translation by ribosomes allows the assembly of amino acids into polypeptides according to the original DNA code. A ribosomal enzyme catalyses peptide bond formation between an amino acid on one tRNA and the growing polypeptide on the other tRNA.
- A ribosome passes along mRNA, one codon at a time, the tRNA with the appropriate anticodon fills the vacant slot and the amino acid forms a peptide bond with the last member of the chain until a stop codon is reached.
- A group of ribosomes moving along one after the other is called a **polysome system**. Each time one ribosome moves along the mRNA a molecule of protein is produced.
- Polypeptides may be further modified and a protein may consist of more than one polypeptide.

Revisit AS notes on the primary, secondary, tertiary and quaternary structure of proteins and how these modifications to the primary structure involve the Golgi body.

Action   1. Draw diagrams to illustrate each stage in the process of protein synthesis.
2. Construct a table to show the functions of DNA, messenger RNA and transfer RNA.

5.1 Meiosis

Meiosis takes place in the reproductive organs of both plants and animals. It results in the formation of gametes with half the normal chromosome number. This is referred to as the haploid number. In contrast to mitosis, meiosis produces cells that are not genetically identical. In fact, meiosis plays an important role in bringing about genetic variation in living organisms.

Meiosis

Meiosis involves two divisions of the cell:
Meiosis I – resulting in two daughter nuclei with half the number of chromosomes of the parent nucleus.
Meiosis II - where the two new haploid nuclei divide again in a division identical to that of mitosis.
The net result is that four haploid nuclei are formed from the parent nucleus.

Like mitosis, meiosis is a continuous process but for convenience it is divided into the four phases of prophase, metaphase, anaphase and telophase, these phases occurring once in each of the two divisions.

When the cell is not dividing it is said to be in interphase. During this phase the DNA content of the cell is doubled and new cell organelles are also formed.

Meiosis I

Prophase I
The chromosomes become shorter and fatter and split into two chromatids. In cells where centrioles are present i.e. animals and lower plants, the **centrioles move to the poles of the cells** and microtubules begin to radiate from them forming asters. This results in the formation of the spindle.
This stage differs from that of mitosis as the paternal and maternal chromosomes **associate in their homologous pairs** and each pair is called a **bivalent.** Each bivalent consists of four strands, made up of two chromosomes, each split into two chromatids. These chromatids wrap around each other and then partially repel each other but remain joined at certain points called **chiasmata.** At these points chromatids may break and recombine with a different but equivalent chromatid. This swapping of pieces of chromosomes is called **crossing over** and is a source of genetic variation.
At the end of prophase the **nuclear membrane disintegrates** and the **nucleolus disappears**.
(Homologous chromosomes carry the same genes at the same positions or loci on the chromosomes but one allele is from the mother and the other from the father. Both alleles may be dominant, or one recessive and one dominant, or both may be recessive. It is the different forms of the same alleles that are exchanged during crossing over).

Metaphase 1
At this stage, when the pairs of homologous chromosomes align themselves on the equator of the spindle, the maternal and paternal chromosomes are arranged randomly. This **random distribution** and consequent **independent assortment** of chromosomes produces **new genetic combinations**.

Anaphase 1

The chromosomes in each bivalent separate and one of each pair is pulled to one pole, its sister chromosome to the opposite pole. Thus each pole receives only **one** of each homologous pair of chromosomes and because of their random arrangement at metaphase these will be a random mixture of maternal and paternal chromosomes. This is called independent assortment of chromosomes and produces new genetic combinations. The chromosomes reach the opposite poles and the **nuclear envelope reforms** around each group of **haploid** chromosomes.

Telophase 1

Usually the chromosomes stay in their condensed form and meiosis II follows on immediately.
In animal cells cytokinesis occurs, that is, the division of the cytoplasm to give two haploid cells.
Many plant cells go straight into meiosis II with no reformation of the spindle.

Meiosis II

Prophase II

The new spindle develops at right angles to the old spindle.

Metaphase II

The chromosomes line up separately on the equator of the spindle, with each chromosome attached to a spindle fibre by its centromere.

Anaphase II

The centromeres divide and the chromatids are pulled to opposite poles.

Telophase II

On reaching the poles the chromatids lengthen and are indistinct. The spindle disappears and the nuclear membrane reforms. Cytokinesis takes place.
The result of these two meiotic divisions is that there are four haploid daughter cells and the genetic make up of each cell is different.

The significance of meiosis

Meiosis is the reduction division that occurs during gamete formation in sexually reproducing organisms. In this division the **diploid** number of chromosomes (2n) is reduced to the **haploid** (n). Thus, when two gametes join together at fertilisation the zygote that is formed has two complete sets of chromosomes returning to the diploid condition. However, meiosis does more than halve the number of chromosomes into a cell, it also introduces genetic variation into the gametes and therefore the zygotes that are produced. The two events that take place during meiosis that help to produce genetic variation are:

- Independent assortment of the homologous chromosomes.
- Crossing over which happens between the chromatids of homologous chromosomes.

When these genetically different gametes fuse, randomly, at fertilisation, more variation is produced amongst the offspring.

In the long term, if a species is to survive in a constantly changing environment and to colonise new environments, sources of variation are essential. There are three ways of creating variety:

- Each of the chromosomes making up a homologous pair carries different genetic material. During sexual reproduction the **genotype of one parent is mixed with that of the other** when haploid gametes fuse.
- The different pairs of **homologous chromosomes** arrange themselves on the spindle during metaphase 1 of meiosis. When they subsequently **separate** they do so entirely **independently** of each other, so that the daughter cells contain different combinations of maternal and paternal chromosomes.
- **Crossing over** during chiasmata formation during prophase 1 of meiosis. Equivalent parts of homologous chromosomes may be exchanged thus producing new combinations and the separation of linked genes.

5.2 Human Reproduction

In the human reproductive system the gametes are produced in special paired glands called gonads. The male gametes or spermatozoa are produced in the testes and the female gametes or egg cells in the ovaries. You need to study the development of gametes which is known as gametogenesis.

Male reproductive system

The male system consists of a pair of **testes**, contained in an external sac, the **scrotum**; the **penis**, which is an intromittent organ; genital ducts connecting the two; and various accessory glands which provide constituents for the semen. Each testis consists of about a thousand **seminiferous tubules** which produce the spermatozoa. The seminiferous tubules also contain interstitial cells that produce the male hormone, testosterone. When sperm have been produced they collect in the vasa efferentia and then pass to the head of the **epididymis** where they mature. They then pass along the coiled tube to the base of the epididymis where they are stored for a short time before passing via the **vas deferens** to the urethra during ejaculation. Before the vas deferens joins the urethra it combines with the duct leading from the **seminal vesicle** to form the ejaculatory duct. The seminal vesicles produce a mucus secretion which helps the mobility of the soerm. The ejaculatory duct then passes through the **prostate gland** which produces an alkaline secretion that neutralises the acidity of any urine in the urethra as well as aiding sperm mobility.

❏ *Action*   1. Draw a labelled diagram of the male reproductive system.
Annotate the diagram with the functions of the structures above shown in bold.
2. Draw T.S. testis.

Female reproductive system

There are two **ovaries** each of which produces ova or eggs. They are produced in the germinal epithelium where they develop into follicles. Mature follicles migrate back to the surface when their development is complete so that the ova can be shed.
Ova are passed to the **fallopian tube** (oviduct) which conveys them to the **uterus** (womb). The uterus has muscular walls and is lined internally by a mucus membrane called the **endometrium**. It is well supplied with blood and is part of the womb into which the embyo implants during pregnancy and which is shed during menstruation. The uterus opens into the **vagina** through a ring of muscle, the cervix.

❏ *Action*   Draw a labelled diagram of the female reproductive system.
Annotate the diagram with the functions of the structures above shown in bold.

Gametogenesis

The production of gametes in the gonads is known as gametogenesis.
* Spermatogenesis is the formation of sperm in the testis.
* Oogenesis is the formation of eggs or ova in the ovary.

The cells of the germinal epithelium of both the testis and the ovary undergo a sequence of mitotic and meiotic divisions to form haploid gametes. It is important that the gametes are haploid so that at fertilisation the diploid number is restored.
First there is a multiplication stage which involves repeated mitotic divisions to produce **spermatogonia** and **oogonia**. Once formed they grow to full size and then undergo maturation which involves meiotic division, and then differentiation into the mature gametes.

Spermatogenesis is the process by which spermatozoa are produced. This takes place in the germinal epithelium of the seminiferous tubule.

- ✓ The diploid spermatogonia divide many times by mitosis to produce **primary spermatocytes.**
- ✓ These then undergo meiosis and after the first meiotic division form haploid **secondary spermatocytes**.
- ✓ After the second meiotic division they form **spermatids** which differentiate into mature **spermatozoa**.

In the wall of the seminiferous tubule are the **Sertoli cells**. They secrete a fluid which nourishes the spermatids and protects them from the immune system of the male.
There are also groups of interstitial cells which secrete the male sex hormone.

❑ *Action*   Draw a labelled diagram to illustrate spermatogenesis.

Oogenesis is the process by which ova are produced in the ovary.
- ✓ **Oogonia**, which are formed before birth, undergo mitosis to form **primary oocytes.**
- ✓ The primary oocytes start to divide by meiosis but the process stops at prophase I.
- ✓ The germinal epithelium also divides to form follicle cells which surround the primary oocytes to form primary follicles.
- ✓ (The primary oocytes do not mature until just before ovulation. About two million of these are formed in the ovary of the foetus but only about 450 will later develop into **secondary oocytes** after the onset of puberty.)
- ✓ At puberty hormones stimulate the follicles to develop further. Each month several follicles start to develop but only one matures into a fully developed Graafian follicle.
- ✓ First the **primary oocyte** completes the first meiotic division to form the haploid **secondary oocyte** and a small polar body.
- ✓ The mature Graafian follicle migrates to the surface of the ovary where it bursts and the secondary oocyte is released, a process called ovulation.
- ✓ The secondary oocyte begins the secondary meiotic division but this is arrested as metaphase unless fertilisation takes place. On fertilisation this division is completed to form a large **ovum** and a second polar body. Once this division has taken place the nucleus of the ovum fuses with that of the sperm to form a **zygote** which will then develop into an **embryo**.

❑ *Action*   1. Draw a labelled diagram to illustrate oogenesis.
             2. Draw a labelled diagram of an ovary showing the stages in development of a follicle.

Recent experiments with mice suggest that oogonia may continue to be produced after birth. If this is true for humans this has important implications for the treatment of sub-fertility.

Sexual intercourse

So that fertilisation can take place the sperm has to travel from the seminiferous tubule to the oviduct of the female. Secretions from the seminal vesicles, Cowper's glands and the prostrate gland, are added to the sperm to form semen.
The penis of a sexually excited male becomes erect as blood under pressure fills the spongy 'erectile tissue'. The vagina of a sexually excited female widens and becomes lubricated by the secretion of mucus. During sexual intercourse the penis is inserted into the vagina. Movements of the penis result in the ejaculation of semen into the vagina. The force of ejaculation is sufficient to propel some sperm through the cervix into the uterus, with the remainder being deposited at the top of the vagina. The sperm swim through the uterus into the oviducts by the lashing movements of their tails. However, only a small proportion (i.e. several hundreds) of the 400 million sperm actually reach the site of fertilization in the oviduct and surround the ovum.

Fertilisation

Internal fertilisation ensures that the sperm are deposited in the female's reproductive tract. From here the sperm use their tails to swim through the cervix and up through the uterus to the oviduct. The sperm can remain viable for 48 hours. If ovulation has recently taken place there will be a secondary oocyte in the oviduct. (The egg or ovum released from the Graafian follicle of the ovary dies within 24 hours unless fertilised.) The secondary oocyte is surrounded by the follicle cells and a clear membrane called the zona pellucida. Several hundred sperm surround the secondary oocyte but only one will penetrate it. When a sperm fuses with an egg cell a diploid zygote is formed. This develops by mitosis to form a mass of cells. This ball of cells is implanted in the uterus wall where it continues to develop.

The acrosome reaction

Sperm can remain viable for 12 to 24 hours after release into the female tract but can fertilise an ovum only after a process called **capacitation** has taken place. This process takes several hours.
It involves changes in the membrane covering the **acrosome**, a thin cap over the nucleus of the sperm. When the sperm reach an oocyte, contact with the zona pellucida results in the acrosome membrane rupturing and protease enzymes are released. The enzymes soften the layers of cells surrounding the oocyte. Inversion of the acrosome results in a fine needle-like filament developing at the tip of the sperm and this pierces the already softened portion of the membrane. The whole process is called the **acrosome reaction** and it enables the sperm to penetrate the egg. This entry stimulates reactions of the oocyte that brings about the formation of the **fertilisation membrane** preventing the entry of further sperm. Entry of the sperm also stimulates the completion of the second meiotic division of the oocyte nucleus. The nuclei of the ovum and sperm are drawn together and fuse to form a diploid nucleus.

❑ *Action*   1. Draw a labelled diagram of a mature sperm cell.
2. Describe the events which occur during fertilisation, including digestion of corona radiata and zona pellucida by acrosomal enzymes, entry of sperm head into secondary oocyte, change in zona pellucida preventing entry of further sperm, second meiotic division to produce female gamete, fusion of nuclei to form zygote.

Implantation

After fertilisation the ovum or zygote begins to divide by mitosis until a hollow ball of cells, the **blastocyst**, is produced. The development of the zygote continues during its passage down the fallopian tube. After about three days the blastocyst reaches the uterus and embeds in the endometrium. This is called **implantation.**
The outer layer of the blastocyst is called the trophoblast. This layer develops into two membranes, the amnion and chorion, the latter of which grows a number of finger-like processes called chorionic villi. The villi increase the surface area for the absorption of nutrients from the wall of the uterus. The chorion also secretes a hormone called human chorionic gonadotrophin (hCG) which prevents the degeneration of the corpus luteum. (This is a structure which develops from the Graafian follicle after the ovum has been released and is important in hormone production during the early stages of pregnancy).
Detection of hCG in the urine is the basis of most pregnancy tests.
The chorionic villi eventually form part of the placenta which is attached to the foetus by the umbilical cord.

Sub-fertility

In the UK, one in six couples trying for a baby, seek medical help because of difficulty in becoming pregnant. Sub-fertility is defined as difficulty in conceiving naturally for reasons affecting the male, female or both partners. Infertility is the complete inability to conceive a child. This is very rare.
The greatest cause of female infertility is the failure to ovulate and is usually associated with absence of, or an irregular menstrual cycle. 95% of cases are treatable with the use of a drug called clomiphene.
Another cause of female infertility is a blockage of the fallopian tubes. This prevents the passage of the ovum to the site of fertilisation in the fallopian tubes. A blockage may be caused by infection and treatment usually involves microsurgery.

Pregnancy testing

Most pregnancy testing kits use monoclonal antibodies to test for the presence of hCG in urine. A monoclonal antibody is one that responds to only one foreign antigen. The monoclonal antibody used in the kits is specific to the hormone, hCG.

Pregnancy testing kits involve the detection of hCG produced by the placenta during the early stages of pregnancy. The hormone is excreted in the urine and high levels act as a confirmation of pregnancy.
The test relies on the reaction between antibodies bound to coloured latex beads and hCG. It causes the hCG molecules to bind together and produce a colour change.
The kit contains a dipstick, which is a strip of absorbent material on a plastic backing in which are embedded the antibodies. The dipstick is placed into a sample of early morning urine and any hCG in the urine will bind to the antibodies at the end of the stick, and will be carried upwards as the urine seeps up the stick. When the hCG – antibody complex reach the test region in the stick, they bind with the immobilised antibodies there and are held firmly in position. As the immobilised antibody complex becomes more and more concentrated there is a colour build-up. If the test is positive a coloured band becomes visible through a transparent window.

❑   **Action**   Draw a labelled diagram to illustrate the reaction in a pregnancy testing kit.

5.3 Sexual reproduction in plants

The flowering plants or angiosperms are the most successful of all terrestrial plants. The flower is the organ of reproduction and usually contains both male and female parts. In angiosperms the female part, the ovule, is never exposed but is enclosed within a modified leaf, the carpel. A key feature of the success of flowering plants is their relationship with animals. Pollen grains have no power of independent movement and have to be transferred to the female part of the flower to ensure fertilisation. Flowering plants have evolved the strategy of attracting animals, particularly insects, to their flowers, feeding them and exploiting their mobility to transfer pollen from flower to flower. Some plants are pollinated by the action of wind.

Flower structure

Flowering plants are diploid and meiosis takes place within the reproductive tissues to produce haploid reproductive structures or spores.
  - ✓ Meiosis takes place in the anther to produce the male spores or pollen grains which contain haploid gametes.
  - ✓ The female spores are the ovules, which are made in the ovary. The female gametes develop inside the ovule.

  - Flowering plants must transfer the pollen grains from the male anther to the female part of a plant of the same species. This is called **pollination**. A pollen grain has a tough resistant wall to prevent it from drying out during this transfer. When the male and female gametes fuse it is called **fertilisation**. The fertilised ovule becomes the seed.
  - The design of a flower is related to its method of pollination. Insect pollinated flowers have, amongst other features, bright colours and a scent, whereas wind pollinated flowers, such as grasses, tend to be green and have no scent.
  - ❖ The following describes the structure of a typical **insect-pollinated flower.**

A flower is made up of four sets of modified leaves arranged from the outside to the centre:
- The outermost ring of structures is the **sepals.** They are usually green and protect the flower in bud.
- Inside the sepals is the ring of **petals**. These are brightly coloured to attract insects. They usually have a scent and may produce nectar, again to attract insects.
- Inside the petals are the male parts of the plant, the **stamens**. Each stamen consists of a long **filament** at the end of which are the **anthers** which produce pollen grains. As well as supporting the anther the filament contains vascular tissue which transports food materials necessary for the formation of pollen grains. The anther is usually made up of four pollen sacs arranged in two pairs, side by side. When mature the pollen sacs split to release the pollen.
- In the centre of the flower are one or more **carpels**. These are the female part of the flower. Each carpel is a closed structure inside which one or more **ovules** develop. The lower part of the carpel, which surrounds the ovules, is called the **ovary** and bears at its apex a stalk-like structure, the **style**. This ends in a receptive surface, the **stigma**.

❑ *Action*   Draw a labelled diagram to show the structure of a named insect-pollinated flower. Annotate the diagram to show the function of the various parts.

❖ **Wind-pollinated flowers** are dull, unattractive and without scent. The petals are usually absent leaving the anthers and stigmas exposed.

❑ *Action*   Draw a labelled diagram of a wind-pollinated flower. e.g. Rye grass (*Lolium perenne*).

Table comparing insect and wind pollinated flowers.

Insect pollinated flowers	Wind pollinated flowers
Colourful petals, scent and nectar	Small, green and inconspicuous, no scent, petals usually absent
Anthers within the flower	Anthers hanging outside the flower
Stigma within the flower	Large, feathery stigmas
Small quantities of sticky pollen	Large quantities of small, smooth, light pollen

❑ **Action** Explain how the features are related to the method of pollination.

Pollination

Pollination is the transfer of pollen grains from the anther to the stigma of a plant of the same species. Pollination is necessary so that the pollen grains, containing the male gametes, are brought into contact with the female part of the flower so that fertilisation can be achieved. This means that pollen grains must be transferred from the ripe anther to the receptive stigma.

Self-pollination
In some species self-pollination occurs and the pollen from the anthers of a flower need only be transferred to the stigma of the **same flower or another flower on the same plant**.

Cross-pollination
In a large number of species cross-pollination occurs where pollen is transferred from the anthers of one flower to the stigma of another flower on **another plant of the same species.**
Flowers are highly adapted for cross pollination by either insects or wind.

In insect pollination, for example, bees feed on the sugary nectar using their long tongues to reach the nectaries at the base of the female part of the flower. As the bee enters the flower, the anthers brush against the back of the bee leaving the sticky pollen behind. When the bee enters another flower, it brushes some of the pollen against the ripe stigma and cross pollination has taken place.

In wind pollinated flowers the anthers hang outside the flower so that the wind can blow away the small, smooth and light pollen. The feathery stigmas hang outside the flowers and provide a large surface area for catching pollen grains that are blown into their path.

Pollination, fertilisation and germination

Self pollination can be an advantage to plants if there are no similar plants nearby. However, it results in in-breeding which results in a reduction in the amount of variation in the population. There will also be a greater chance of two undesirable recessive alleles being brought together at fertilisation.

Therefore the two forms of pollination have very different genetic consequences:
- Self-pollination leads to self-fertilisation, cross-pollination to cross-fertilisation.
- Self-fertilised species depend on random assortment and crossing over during meiosis, and on mutation to bring about variation in the genomes of male and female gametes.
- Self-fertilised species therefore display less genetic variation than cross-fertilised species that are produced from gametes from two different individuals.
- There are advantages to inbreeding because it can preserve good genomes which may be suited to a relatively stable environment. Out-breeding is of greater evolutionary significance because in the struggle for survival some genomes are more successful than others.

Many flowering plant species have evolved a variety of mechanisms to ensure that cross-pollination takes place, so ensuring out-breeding. Anthers and stigma may mature at different times, they may be at different levels in the flower or there may be separate male and female flowers on different plants.

Fertilisation

- Diploid cells in the **pollen grain** undergo **meiosis** to form haploid cells. Each of these cells develops into a **pollen grain.** This has a thick outer wall, the **exine**, and a thin inner wall, the **intine**.

- *Action* Draw a labelled diagram of a pollen grain

- When the pollen is ripe, the outer layers of the anthers dry out and tensions are set up in lateral grooves. Eventually dehiscence occurs and the edges of the pollen sacs curl away exposing the pollen grains. In insect pollinated flowers these will be carried to the stigma by insects, such as bees.

- A diploid cell in the **ovule** undergoes **meiosis** to form a haploid cell.

- *Action* Draw a diagram to show a mature ovule within the carpel and label the following structures; integuments, nucleus and micropyle.

Fertilisation is the process where a male gamete fuses with a female gamete to produce a zygote. In flowering plants the ovule is protected within the ovary. The male gamete is the nucleus contained in the pollen grain and can only reach the female nucleus in the ovule by means of a pollen tube.
- On landing on the stigma the pollen grains absorb water and germinate producing a pollen tube.
- The pollen tube grows down the style. It secretes enzymes as it goes, digesting its way through the tissues of the style.
- The tip of the pollen tube bursts open releasing the male gamete into an area of the ovule called the embryo sac. This contains the female nucleus.
- As the pollen tube penetrates the embryo sac, the tip opens and the male gamete nucleus enters.
- The male nucleus fuses with the female nucleus to form a zygote.

❏ **Action** Draw a diagram of an ovary containing a single ovule showing a pollen tube as it enters through the micropyle.

Development of the seed and fruit

Following fertilisation the development of the seed and fruit takes place. The seed develops from the fertilised ovule and contains an embryonic plant and a food store.

- The diploid **zygote** divides by **mitosis** to form the embryo, consisting of a **plumule** (developing shoot), a **radicle** (developing root) and one or two seed leaves or **cotyledons**.
- A store of food materials develops to provide reserves for the developing embryo.
- The **ovary** becomes the **fruit.**
- The **ovule** becomes the **seed**.

Structure of the seed

Flowering plants are divided into two main groups, monocotyledons and dicotyledons.
The monocotyledons are important as they include cereals.
The broad bean is classed as a dicotyledon as it has two seed leaves or cotyledons whereas the maize is classed as a monocotyledon as it has only one cotyledon. In the broad bean the food store has been absorbed into the cotyledons but in the maize, typically of cereal grains, the food store surrounds the seed leaves. The maize is in fact a fruit and not a seed.

❏ **Action** 1. Draw a labelled diagram of a broad bean seed (*Vicia faba*) – internal and external. Label – micropyle, testa, position of radicle, plumule, cotyledons.
2. Draw a labelled diagram of the maize fruit (*Zea mays*).

Germination

After a period of dormancy and when environmental factors are favourable stored food will be mobilised and the seed will germinate. The three main requirements for successful germination are:
- a suitable **temperature** – the optimum temperature for germination is the optimum for the enzymes involved in the process of germination. The temperature varies from species to species.
- **water** – needed for the mobilisation of enzymes, vacuolation of cells and for transport.
- **oxygen** – respiration makes energy, in the form of ATP, available for metabolism and growth.

Mobilisation of food reserves during germination

The following describes the germination of the broad bean.
Food reserves in seeds are insoluble in water and cannot as such be transported in the seedling. The reserves must be broken down into relatively simple soluble substances which dissolve in water and are then transported to the growing apices of the young shoot or plumule and the young root or radicle. Water is taken up rapidly by the seed in the initial stages, causing the tissues to swell as well as mobilising the enzymes. The seed coat ruptures as the radicle pushes its way through first. The radicle will grow downwards and the plumule upwards. The enzyme, amylase, hydrolyses starch into maltose which is transported to growing points. During germination the cotyledons of the broad bean remain below ground. The plumule is bent over in the shape of a hook as it pushes its way up through the soil. This protects the tip from damage by soil abrasion. If the seed has been planted at the correct depth in the soil, when the plumule emerges it unfurls and begins to make food for itself by photosynthesis. By now the food reserves in the cotyledons will have been depleted.

5.4 Variability and genetics

Meiosis does more than halve the number of chromosomes in a cell, it also introduces genetic variation. Genetic variation may also arise as a result of mutation. The various sources of variation help to bring about natural selection which has produced the vast range of species that inhabit Earth.

Gregor Mendel (1822-84) was the first person to work out the ways in which genes are inherited. He formulated two laws which form the basis of the science of genetics. This was an amazing feat as scientists of the time had no knowledge of DNA, genes or chromosomes.

Genes and alleles

In 1866 Gregor Mendel suggested that the characteristics of organisms were determined by 'units' which were handed on from generation to generation. Later these units were identified as **genes** which were carried on and transmitted by chromosomes. A gene is the basic unit of inheritance.

Genes consist of DNA and have three main characteristics:
- They can separate and combine.
- They can mutate.
- They code for the production of specific polypeptides.

The definition of a gene based on function is 'one gene being the portion of a chromosome which codes for one polypeptide'.

Alleles are alternative forms of genes occupying a similar gene-position (or 'locus') on homologous chromosomes. If a gene determines a particular inherited characteristic, the alleles which make up the gene may exist in two forms. For example, in a gene which determines fur colour in mice, the two alternative alleles may be for black and white fur. 'Black' and 'white' are the two alleles for the 'fur colour' gene.

For any one locus on a chromosome, there are theoretically three different allele combinations.
- ✓ **heterozygous** – having different alleles for a given gene, that is, a dominant allele and a recessive allele are present together. Each of these alleles is carried on a different chromosome within a pair of homologous chromosomes.
- ✓ **homozygous** dominant – having the same two dominant alleles present for a given gene.
- ✓ **homozygous** recessive - having the same two recessive alleles present for a given gene.

In the simplest situations, a particular characteristic is controlled by a single gene. If an organism is heterozygous for this gene, the dominant allele will determine the form in which the characteristic is actually expressed. The outcome (that is the **phenotype**) of a heterozygous condition (that is, the **genotype**) will therefore be the same as that for a homozygous dominant condition.

Genetic terms
- **Dominant** allele - of the pair of alleles on homologous chromosomes, the one that always produces an effect on the appearance of the organism when present is the dominant allele. It is usually represented by a capital letter e.g. T (for tall).
- **Recessive** allele – the allele that produces an effect only when present as an identical pair is the recessive allele e.g. t (for short).
- **Genotype** – the combination of alleles found in an individual.
- **Phenotype** – the appearance of an organism, determined by the genotype.
- **Homozygous** – if both alleles are the same e.g. TT, tt.
- **Heterozygous** – if the pair of alleles are dissimilar e.g. Tt.
- **F1** – first filial generation; **F2** – second filial generation.

❑ *Action*   1. Distinguish between the following terms: gene and allele; dominant and recessive; genotype and phenotype; homozygous and heterozygous.
2. Draw a labelled diagram of a homologous pair of chromosomes showing alternative alleles for a single gene, such as fur colour in mice.

Monohybrid inheritance

Mendel's early experiments were based on selecting pea plants of two varieties which showed clearly separable characteristics such as tall and dwarf plants and round and wrinkled seeds. From his results he formulated his first law of inheritance, the law of segregation, which states that:

'*The characteristics of an organism are determined by factors (alleles) which occur in pairs. Only one of a pair of factors (alleles) can be present in a single gamete*'.

The inheritance of a single pair of contrasting characters is known as **monohybrid inheritance.**

In monohybrid crosses, two heterozygous individuals will produce offspring with a phenotypic ratio of three dominant to one recessive.

Instructions for carrying out a genetic cross

(*Once you have practised a number of crosses it is very easy to miss out stages or explanations. This may make your explanations impossible for others to follow. In an exam, even if you achieve the expected outcome, you may not gain full credit. So always carry out these instructions in their entirety*).

1. Look carefully at the information you are given in the question, e.g. about phenotypes of the parents, whether they are homozygous or heterozygous.
2. Choose suitable symbols for the alleles, unless they are provided in the question.
   a) Choose a single letter to represent each characteristic.
   b) Choose the first letter of one of the contrasting features.
   c) If possible, choose a letter in which the higher and lower case forms differ in shape as well as size.
   d) Let the higher case letter represent the dominant feature and the lower case letter the recessive one.
3. Represent the parents with the appropriate pairs of letters. Label them clearly as 'parents' and state their phenotypes.
4. State the gametes produced by each parent. Circle the gametes and label them clearly.
5. Use a matrix, called a Punnett square, to show the results of the random crossing of the gametes.
6. State the phenotype of each different genotype and indicate the numbers of each type.
7. Make sure that you have actually answered the question.

❑ ***Action***   Draw a genetic diagram to show the outcome of a cross between tall pea plants crossed with short pea plants. Use suitable symbols, to include F1 and F2 generations.

Mendel was lucky in his choice of characters in pea plants because these particular characters are controlled by single genes. Pea plants are either tall or dwarf, flower colours are clear-cut and easy to tell apart. This is an example of discontinuous variation. However, most characters are controlled by a number of genes, for instance height in humans. People are not just tall or short but show a range of heights. This is an example of continuous variation.

Test cross

The 'backcross' or test cross is a method used in genetics to determine whether a particular dominant characteristic observed in an organism is determined by one or two dominant alleles.

For example, a mouse with black fur could be homozygous dominant (BB) or heterozygous (Bb). The appearance of the black fur (phenotype) is identical in both cases.

The backcross consists of a 'cross' (that is, cross fertilisation) between an unknown 'dominant' genotype and a known 'recessive' genotype. (The double recessive phenotype has a known genotype because only one allele combination can produce it).

❑ ***Action***   Draw two genetic diagrams to show how a backcross can reveal the genotype of a plant having a dominant phenotype (tall).

Dihybrid inheritance

Dihybrid inheritance involves the inheritance of **two** separate genes. Mendel knew from his early experiments with monohybrid crosses that round seed shape was dominant to wrinkled, and that yellow colour was dominant to green. He used plants which differed by having two pairs of contrasting characters. He crossed homozygous pea plants with the two dominant characters, round and yellow seeds with homozygous plants with the two recessive characters, wrinkled and green.

- Homozygous plants with round and yellow seeds were crossed with homozygous plants with wrinkled and green seeds.
- He found that all the F1 generation had round, yellow seeds.
- When plants grown from these seeds were self-pollinated the seeds produced were of **four** different types of shape and colour of seed coat.
- He collected and counted the seeds and found there were four types as shown in the table.

characteristic	Round, yellow	Round, green	Wrinkled, yellow	Wrinkled, green
totals	315	108	101	32

Each total can be divided by the double recessive total to give an approximate whole number ratio between the phenotypes, i.e. 9:3:3:1 is the ratio between the four totals in the table.
The ratio proportions are known as the dihybrid ratio.
This led Mendel to formulate his second law, which states that:
'Either one of a pair of contrasted characters may combine with either of another pair'.
With our present knowledge of genetics this statement can be rewritten as:
'Each member of an allelic pair may combine randomly with either of another pair'.

- ❑ **Action**   Draw a genetic diagram to show the outcome of a cross between round green seeds and wrinkled yellow seeds. Use suitable symbols, to include F1 and F2 generations.

Probability

The presentation of a breeding experiment, such as that shown in the 'Action' above, is a prediction of the likely outcome. What is actually observed may not agree precisely with the prediction. Consider the situation where a coin is tossed 100 times. It would be expected to land heads on 50 occasions and tails on 50 occasions. In practice it would be unusual to obtain this result the first 100 attempts. If the coin lands 60 heads and 40 tails, is this due to a chance deviation from the expected result or is the coin biased in some way?
The following description is to aid your understanding that the results of conventional genetic crosses are due to chance. You would not be required to reproduce this description in a theory exam.

If two unbiased coins are tossed there are four possible combinations:
$$HH \text{ or } HT \text{ or } TH \text{ or } TT.$$
- Rule of addition:
  Consider one of the coins. When this is tossed it is certain to give either H or T. Thus the probability of getting either one result or another result is obtained by *adding* their independent probabilities. The probability of getting H is ½ and the probability of getting T is also ½.
  Thus the probability of getting one or the other is
  $$½ + ½ = 1 \text{ or } 100\% \text{ certainty.}$$

- Rule of multiplication:
  Now consider both coins. The probability that there will be H on both the first and the second coin is obtained by multiplying the two independent probabilities. In this case the probability of getting H on the first coin is ½ , and the probability of getting H on the second coin is also ½.
  Thus the probability of HH is ½ x ½ = ¼.

The result of your Punnett square for a monohybrid cross shows a 3:1 ratio in the appearance of dominant and recessive F2 phenotypes. This can be used to calculate the probability of the cross when the four alleles, round, green, yellow and wrinkled are involved.

- the probability of the four alleles appearing in any of the F2 offspring is:

  round (dominant) ¾   yellow (dominant) ¾
  wrinkled (recessive) ¼   green (recessive) ¼

- The probability of combinations of alleles appearing in the F2 is as follows:
  ✓ round and yellow = ¾ x ¾ = 9/16
  ✓ round and green = ¾ x ¼ = 3/16
  ✓ wrinkled and yellow = ¼ x ¾ = 3/16
  ✓ wrinkled and green = ¼ x ¼ = 1/16

Chi squared test (X^2)

Looking back at Mendel's dihybrid cross the expected ratio of phenotypes in the offspring is 9:3:3:1. This ratio represents the probability of getting these phenotypes. It would be surprising if the numbers came out exactly in this ratio. So how close do the observed results have to be to the expected and have the differences between them happened by chance, or are they so different that something unexpected is taking place?

To answer this question scientists use a statistical test called the Chi-squared test.

The Chi^2 test is used to compare the observed results with those expected. It is a way of estimating the probability that differences between observed and expected results are due to chance alone and not some other factor influencing the results. Statisticians carry out the following procedure:

1. Calculate the expected values (E). In the table on the previous page this is the total number of seeds divided by the number of possible types, that is $\frac{556 \times 9}{16}$ etc .

    These have been filled in the 'expected' column in the table below.

2. Calculate the differences between the observed (O) and expected (E) results.

3. Square the differences.

4. Use the formula $= \sum \frac{(O-E)^2}{E}$

5. Check the figures in the table.

phenotype	Observed (O)	Expected (E)	Difference (O-E)	$(O-E)^2$	$\frac{(O-E)^2}{E}$
Round yellow	313	311	2.0	4	0.01
Round green	108	104	-4.0	16	0.15
Wrinkled yellow	101	104	-3.0	9	0.08
Wrinkled green	32	35	3.0	9	0.26

$$X^2 = 0.50$$

6. Work out the degrees of freedom. This is a measure of the spread of the data. It is always one less than the number of classes of data. In the example there are four different phenotype combinations, so there are three degrees of freedom.

7. To find out if this value is significant or non significant it is necessary to use a chi- squared table.

Number of classes	Degrees of freedom	Chi^2			
2	1	0.00	0.45	2.71	3.84
3	2	0.02	1.39	4.61	5.99
4	3	0.12	2.37	6.25	7.82
5	4	0.30	3.36	7.78	9.49
Probability that deviation is due to chance alone		0.99(99%)	0.5(50%)	0.10(10%)	0.05(5%)

Statisticians consider that if the probability is greater than 5% the deviation is said to be non significant. In other words, the deviation is due to chance alone. If the deviation is less than the 5% level the deviation is said to be significant. That is, some factor other than chance is influencing the results.

8. Looking along the column for three degrees of freedom it can be seen that the Chi^2 value of 0.50 lies between 2.37 and 0.12 which is equivalent to a probability between 0.50 (50%) and 0.99 (99%). This means that the deviation from the 9:3:3:1 ratio is non significant and is simply the result of statistical chance.

Not all characteristics are controlled by single genes which behave independently, as was the case in Mendel's experiments. You need to know about codominance (monohybrid only), how sex is determined and how genes on sex chromosomes cause unexpected ratios.

Codominance

The monohybrid and dihybrid crosses considered so far involve alleles that are either dominant or recessive. Sometimes both alleles are expressed and neither is dominant.

When alleles express themselves equally in the phenotype this is known as codominance. In most cases the heterozygote shows a phenotype intermediate between those of the two homozygotes.

Examples of codominance are:

- Snapdragon plants have the homozygous genotypes RR and WW and produce red or white flowers. However, if the two homozygous plants are crossed, the offspring are pink. That is, the two parents produce an intermediate offspring.
- Similarly, shorthorn cattle have the genotypes and phenotypes RR (red), RW (roan) and WW (white) coat colour.

The genetic diagram for these crosses is the same as that illustrating Mendel's first law but in the F1 all individuals have the intermediate phenotype.

❏ **Action**   Draw a genetic diagram to show the outcome of a cross between a homozygous red shorthorn bull and a white shorthorn cow. Use suitable symbols to include the F1.

(Where codominance is involved it is usual to use different letters to represent each allele, e.g. R to represent red and W to represent white. So the F1 would be shown as RW.)

Sex determination

Most sexually reproducing animals show two morphologically distinct types, male and female, which are associated with the chromosomes found in the two types. One pair, known as the **sex chromosomes**, is similar in one sex and dissimilar in the other. The non-sex chromosomes are known as **autosomes.**

- Humans have 46 chromosomes arranged in 23 pairs. The first 22 pairs are the autosomes, the last pair are the sex chromosomes.
- The male has dissimilar chromosomes, called **X** and **Y**, whilst the female has two similar **X** chromosomes.
- All the female's eggs contain an X chromosome.
- Half the male's sperm contain an X chromosome and the other half contain a Y chromosome.
- At fertilisation the egg may join with either an X sperm or a Y sperm. This gives an equal chance of the child being a boy or a girl.

❏ **Action**   Draw a simple genetic diagram to illustrate the determination of sex.

Sex-linked inheritance

Some alleles are carried on the X chromosome, so they are described as sex linked.
The Y chromosome is much smaller than the X and carries very few genes.
Therefore in the male any recessive genes carried on the X chromosome will express themselves in the phenotype. This is because they are unpaired and so there is no dominant gene present. This special form of inheritance is known as **sex-linkage**, an important feature of which is that the male cannot hand on the gene to his sons as they must receive the Y chromosome to become male. On the other hand, all his daughters must receive the recessive gene from him. Females who are heterozygous for sex-linked recessive traits are known as carriers and have a 50% chance of handing on the recessive to their sons.

An example of a sex-linked trait in humans is **haemophilia**.
It is caused by a recessive allele on the X chromosome.
The gene that codes for Factor VIII, an important protein involved in blood clotting, is a sex-linked gene located on the X chromosome.

*   Haemophilia is a potentially lethal condition. It is the result of an individual being unable to produce one of the many clotting factors. The inability of the blood to clot leads to slow and persistent bleeding.
*   It is now possible to extract the particular clotting factor from donated blood allowing haemophiliacs to lead near-normal lives. (Although the risk of passing the disease on to their children remains).
*   This condition occurs almost exclusively in males.
*   When the recessive allele occurs in males it expresses itself because the Y chromosome cannot carry any corresponding dominant allele.
*   For the condition to arise in females it requires the double recessive state and as the recessive allele is relatively rare in the population this is unlikely to occur.
*   To obtain an affected female, the father must be affected and the mother either affected or a carrier.

If   H is the allele for normal blood clotting
     h is the allele for haemophilia
     an individual could have the genotype

$X^H X^H$ female, normal
$X^H X^h$ female carrier
$X^h X^h$ female, haemophiliac
$X^H Y$ male, normal
$X^h Y$ male, haemophiliac

❏ ***Action***   1.Construct a genetic diagram to show the outcome of a cross between a man who does not have haemophilia and a woman who carries the allele for haemophilia. Describe the phenotypes of the offspring. What is the probability of a son being a haemophiliac? What is the probability of a daughter being a carrier?
2. Construct a genetic diagram to show the outcome of a cross between a carrier mother and a haemophiliac father.

Don't forget to include all the stages for carrying out a genetic cross listed on page (15).

Linkage

In living organisms, the number of chromosomes in each cell varies and is usually less than 50. However, each chromosome consists of many genes and may be thought of as a linear sequence of genes that are all linked together. Genes on the same chromosome will tend to be inherited together. The crosses and ratios considered so far have involved two pairs of contrasting characters found on *different* chromosomes. These ratios will not be obtained if the genes are found on the *same* chromosome.

Linkage takes place when two different genes are located on the same chromosome. The genes are inherited together, because they move together during meiosis and appear in the same gamete.

Recombination takes place when alleles are exchanged between homologous chromosomes as a result of crossing over. The further apart two genes are on a chromosome, the more chance there is of crossing over taking place.

o   **Action**   Insert a diagram to illustrate crossing over.

The new combinations are the result of crossing over in prophase I of meiosis. These new combinations are called recombinants.

Mutations

A mutation is an unpredictable change in the genetic material of an organism. Mutations create completely new alleles and are an important source of genetic variation. There are two types of mutation, gene mutations and chromosome mutations.

Mutations

A mutation is a change in the amount, arrangement or structure in the DNA of an organism.
- It may affect a single gene or a whole chromosome.
- Most mutations occur in somatic (body) cells.
- Only those mutations which occur in the formation of gametes can be inherited.
- Mutations are spontaneous random events which may provide a source of material for natural selection pressures and therefore evolution.
- Mutations rates are normally very small, therefore mutation has less impact on evolution than other sources of variation (the average rate at which a mutation occurs is about 1 in 100,000).
- In general, organisms with short life cycles and more frequent meiosis show a greater rate of mutation.
- The rate of mutations occurring can be increased by ionising radiation and mutagenic chemicals.

Mutagens and the mutation rate.

Mutations happen naturally. However, scientists have found that the mutation rate is increased if organisms are exposed to mutagens. These are factors in the environment which include:
- X-rays, gamma radiation and UV light.
- Chemicals, such as polycyclic hydrocarbons in cigarette smoke.
A mutagen which causes cancer is a carcinogen.
It is incorrect to say that mutagens cause mutations. Increased exposure to mutagens increases the *rate* of mutations occurring.

Mutations can happen in two ways:
- DNA is not copied properly before cell division.
  Sometimes mistakes are made in the copying process so that new chromosomes are faulty. Usually they are small errors, involving only one gene, so they are called **gene mutations** or point mutations. However, this can be a serious problem for the individual if a very important gene is affected.

- Chromosomes are damaged and break.
  If chromosomes break they will normally repair themselves (the DNA will rejoin) but they may not repair themselves correctly. This can lead to large changes in the structure of the DNA and may affect a large number of genes. These are called **chromosome mutations**.

Gene mutations

A change in the structure of a DNA molecule, producing a different allele of a gene, is a gene mutation. Any gene can mutate but rates vary from one gene to another within an organism. Gene mutations are changes in the base pairs within the genes. They can take the form of duplication, insertion, deletion, inversion or substitution of bases. Whatever the change, the result is the formation of a modified polypeptide.

How can mutations cause a change in phenotype?

The genetic code, which ultimately determines an organism's characteristics, is made up of a specific sequence of nucleotides on the DNA molecule. Any change to one or more of these nucleotides, or any rearrangement of the sequence, will produce the incorrect sequence of amino acids in the protein it makes.

The protein made is often an enzyme which may then be unable to catalyse a specific reaction. For example, a specific enzyme is necessary to convert a chemical precursor into the skin pigment, melanin. If a gene mutation results in the inability to produce this enzyme, the organism will lack a pigment. The organism is referred to as an albino.

Sickle cell anaemia

A gene mutation (substitution) in the gene producing haemoglobin results in a defect called **sickle-cell anaemia**. The replacement of just one base in the DNA molecule results in the wrong amino acid being incorporated into two of the polypeptide chains which make up the haemoglobin molecule. The abnormal haemoglobin causes red blood cells to become sickle-shaped, resulting in anaemia and possible death. Haemoglobin S is produced instead of normal haemoglobin by a single base chain that causes valine to be substituted for glutamic acid at the sixth position in the β globulin chain. DNA codes for glutamic acid are CTT or CTC. Two of the codes for valine are CAT and CAC. In either case the substitution of A for T as the second base would bring about the formation of haemoglobin S.

The mutant gene is codominant. In the homozygous state the individual suffers the disease but in the heterozygous state the individual has 30-40 percent sickle cells, the rest are normal. The heterozygous condition is referred to as sickle-cell trait.

Chromosome mutations

Mutations causing changes in the structure or number of whole chromosomes in cells are known as chromosome mutations. They are most likely to occur during meiosis, when the process can go wrong as the paired chromosomes line up on the crowded equator at metaphase and are pulled apart in anaphase. Errors can result in the chromosomes not being shared equally between the daughter cells.

Changes in structure

During prophase I of meiosis, homologous chromosomes pair up and exchange of material takes place at chiasmata. Errors arise when chromosomes rejoin with the corresponding pieces of chromosome on its homologous partner. Often the homologous chromosomes end up with a different gene sequence. This makes it impossible for pairing up in meiosis to take place.
(No details are required but this type of mutation is important as a source of variation).

Changes in numbers

Nondisjunction is a process in which faulty cell division means that one of the daughter cells receives two copies of a chromosome while the other gets none. *In Down's syndrome* chromosome number 21 is affected. If this happens in an ovary, it results in an oocyte with either no chromosome 21 or with two copies instead of one. Oocytes with no chromosome 21 die but those with two copies survive and may be fertilised. The resulting zygote has three chromosome 21's with a total of 47 chromosomes. This condition is known as trisomy 21 and the zygote will develop into a child with Down's syndrome.
Down's syndrome occurs in approximately 1 in 700 births and the incidence of the mutation is related to the age of the mother, a result of the higher chance of mutation occurring during the formation of oocytes in older ovaries. At the age of 20 the risk is 1 in 2000, at 40 years 1 in 100, and after 45 years the risk has risen to 1 in 30. Children with Down's syndrome have open, slightly flattened faces. They are usually happy and friendly but there are varying degrees of mental retardation.

Changes in sets of chromosomes

Occasionally a mutation can affect whole sets of chromosomes. This is known as polyploidy.
A defect in meiosis may result in a gamete receiving two sets of chromosomes. When this diploid gamete is fertilised by a normal haploid gamete the zygote will be triploid, that is, having three sets of chromosomes. If two diploid gametes fuse then a tetraploid will be produced. Tetraploidy may also happen after fertilisation if, during mitosis, the two sets of chromosomes double but fail to separate. Polyploidy is common in flowering plants and is associated with beneficial characteristics. Tomatoes and wheat are polyploids. Triploids are usually sterile as they cannot form homologous pairs.

Why are mutations important?

Mutations are important because they increase variation in a population. Most mutations are harmful to the organism concerned. Beneficial mutations are very rare but they may give a selective advantage to an organism.

- If a mutation is in a body cell, it may cause cancer. For example increased exposure to UV light is linked to skin cancer.
- If the mutation is in a gamete, it will not affect the individual producing the gamete, but will affect the zygote that develops from it, that is, the offspring.
- These mutations cause sudden and distinct differences between individuals. They are therefore the basis of discontinuous variation.
- There are potential advantages from mutations that are beneficial and may increase variation. However, most mutations are recessive to the normal allele. A recessive mutant allele must await replication in the gene pool over many generations before chance brings recessive alleles together, resulting in their expression.

Carcinogens

Substances that cause cancer are called carcinogens. These affect the DNA in cells, resulting in mutations.

Mutations that occur in body or somatic cells often have no effect on an organism. Most mutated cells are recognised as foreign by the body's immune system and are destroyed.
Occasionally the mutation may affect the regulation of cell division. Cancers are thought to start when changes take place in these genes. The term for a mutated gene that causes cancer is an oncogene.

If a cell with such a mutation escapes the attack of the immune system it can produce a lump of cells called a tumour. Tumours are usually harmless or benign but sometimes the tumour cells are able to spread around the body and invade other tissues. This type of tumour is described as malignant and the diseases caused by such tumours are cancers.

Any agent that causes cancer is called a carcinogen and is described as carcinogenic. Therefore some mutagens are carcinogenic.

Smoking and cancer

Tobacco smoke contains a number of harmful chemicals that affect human health. These include tar, nicotine and carbon monoxide. Tar is a mixture of many toxic chemicals. It collects in the lungs as the tobacco smoke cools. Tar contains carcinogens which affect the DNA in the cells of the alveoli. Normally, genes control cell division and division is halted when sufficient cells have been produced for growth and repair. Tumour suppressor genes normally inhibit cell division. Carcinogens in tobacco smoke cause these genes to mutate, so that they do not carry out their normal function, leading to uncontrolled cell division. Oncogenes and mutated suppressor genes can both lead to lung cancer. About 25% of all cancer deaths in developed countries are due to carcinogens in the tar of tobacco smoke.

5.5 Variation and evolution

Sexual reproduction produces genetic variation amongst individuals in a population. In the long term, if a species is to survive in a constantly changing environment and to colonise new environments, sources of variation are essential. The genotype of an organism gives it the potential to show a particular characteristic. The degree to which the characteristic is shown is also affected by the organism's environment.

Types of variation

Most characters are controlled by a number of genes and the differences in the character are not clear-cut. A character within a population which shows a gradation from one extreme to another shows **continuous variation**, for example, height. If an individual has inherited a number of alleles for tallness from the parents, that individual has the potential to grow tall. However, if the individual has a poor diet he may not develop to his full potential. Usually the differences have to be measured to tell the phenotypes apart.

Characters that are clear-cut and easy to tell apart are controlled by a single gene. When these types of differences occur it is known as **discontinuous variation.** This gene may have two or more alleles. There are no intermediate types. For example, light and dark forms in some moth species.

Origins of variation

Non-heritable variation

The environment has a role in determining phenotypic variation. Environmental factors in humans may include diet and exercise whereas plants are affected by temperature, light and available nutrients.

An organism will inherit genes, giving it a theoretical maximum size, but whether or not this is reached will depend upon nutrition during the growth period and other environmental factors. Thus, if organisms of identical genotype are subject to different environmental influences, they show considerable variety. Because these influences are varied, they are largely responsible for continuous variation in a population. This is known as **non-heritable variation.**

Heritable variation

Variations due to the effect of the environment have little evolutionary significance as they are not passed from one generation to the next. Much more important to evolution is **inherited variation** that results from genetic changes. As a result of sexual reproduction, variation may be increased when the genotype of one parent is mixed with that of the other. The sexual process has three inbuilt methods of creating variety:

- The mixing of two different parental genotypes where cross-fertilisation occurs.
- The random distribution of chromosomes during metaphase I of meiosis.
- The crossing over between homologous chromosomes during prophase I of meiosis.

Although these processes may establish a new combination of alleles in one generation it is **mutations** that generate long-lasting variation of a novel kind. However, as previously stated, the occurrence of a useful mutation is a very rare event.

Overproduction

All organisms have the reproductive potential to increase their populations, although they rarely do so. As a population increases various environmental factors come into play to keep the numbers down. In other words, organisms must compete for limited resources. For example, plants compete for light, space, mineral ions etc.; animals compete for food, shelter etc.

Consider a population of rabbits. The female may produce several litters each year with a number of young in each litter. If all the young rabbits survived to become adults and they, in turn, reproduced, then the rabbit population would increase rapidly. Eventually, as the increasing number of rabbits eat an increasing amount of vegetation such as grass, food would become in short supply. Overcrowding would take place allowing diseases to spread. Predators, such as foxes, would increase. These environmental factors act to reduce the rate of growth of the rabbit population. Only a small proportion of the young rabbits will develop into adults and reproduce so population growth slows. Over a period of time the population will oscillate about a mean level.

To summarise:

The number of young produced is far greater than the number which will survive to become adults. Many young die before maturity and so do not reproduce. Two types of competition are apparent:

- Competition between individuals of the same species (intra-specific competition). This is the basis of the origin of species by natural selection.
- Competition between individuals of different species (inter-specific competition) is illustrated by predator-prey relationships.

Selection pressure

What determines which individuals die and which survive?

Is it a matter of luck or are some individuals born with a better chance of survival than others. Variation within a population of organisms means that some will have characteristics which give them an advantage in the 'struggle for survival'.

In rabbits coat colour may vary. Most rabbits have alleles which give the normal brown colour. A small number may be homozygous for the recessive allele which gives a white coat. A white rabbit will stand out and is more likely to be killed by a predator, such as a fox. As the white rabbit is unlikely to survive to become a mature adult, the chances of it reproducing and passing on its allele for white coat are very small. The allele for white coat will remain rare in the population. However, in the arctic winter the disadvantage becomes an advantage.

Predation by foxes is an example of a selection pressure. Selection pressures increase the chances of some alleles being passed on to the next generation, and decrease the chance of others being passed on. The effect of such selection pressures on the frequency of alleles in a population is called natural selection. Predation increases 'fitness' in the prey. For example foxes kill the weakest rabbits.

Selection, in the context of evolution, is the process by which organisms that are better adapted to their environment survive and breed, while those less well adapted fail to do so. These better adapted organisms are more likely to pass on their characteristics to succeeding generations. The organism's environment exerts a **selection pressure** and this determines the spread of any allele within the gene pool.

5.5 Population genetics

Organisms are members of a local population in which mating occurs at random. The study of the inheritance of factors in a population is concerned with the **frequency** of phenotypes and genotypes of the whole population rather than the ratios of characteristics among offspring examined in Mendelian studies. A population is a group of organisms that can freely interbreed. Some populations are 'open' with immigration of genes from overlapping populations. Other populations are 'closed' populations cut off by barriers. In any of these populations the total of their genes located in reproductive cells make up the gene pool.

Gene pool

Population genetics is concerned with determining the relative proportions of the various genotypes present in a population, from which can be calculated the relative proportions of alleles in the population. This is known as allele frequency.

A population of organisms reproducing sexually contains a large amount of genetic variation called a **gene pool.** Each organism contains just one of the many possible sets of genes that can be formed from the pool. The gene pool remains stable if the environment is stable. However, if the environment changes some phenotypes will be advantageous and will be selected for, whilst others will be disadvantageous and will be selected against. Thus a gene pool is constantly changing, some alleles becoming more frequent and others less frequent. In some circumstances alleles may be totally lost from the gene pool.

The Hardy-Weinberg principle states that in a large, randomly mating population, assuming the absence of migration, mutation and selection, the gene and genotype frequencies remain constant. That is, the proportion of dominant and recessive alleles of a particular gene remains the same. It is not altered by interbreeding.

One useful application of the Hardy-Weinberg principle is that if the frequency of one of the alleles in a gene pool is known, the Hardy-Weinberg equation can be used to calculate the expected proportions of the genotypes in the population.

The Hardy-Weinberg Law demonstrates that a large proportion of recessive alleles exist in the heterozygotes. Heterozygotes are a reservoir of genetic variability.

(*The Hardy-Weinberg principle is not specifically on the syllabus and so will not be required in an exam. However, your teacher may use it to help explain this topic*).

The Hardy-Weinberg principle is used to calculate allele and genotype frequencies in a population. It can therefore be used to predict the number of defective individuals in a population.
The Hardy-Weinberg equation may be expressed as follows:

$$p^2 + 2pq + q^2 = 1$$

Consider a pair of alleles Aa; let p = frequency of A, and q = frequency of a.
In the population $p + q = 1$.

Assuming random mating then in the next generation
$AA = p^2$; $Aa = 2pq$; $aa = q^2$.

Consider the following example:
A recessive allele confers resistance to an insecticide in a particular insect species. Explain how the allele is distributed if 36% of the insect population is resistant.

Allele frequency is represented as a decimal fraction.
Since a gene has two alleles, their combined frequency = 1.

rr = 36 % or 0.36   i.e. q^2 = 0.36   q = 0.36 = 0.6
Since p + q = 1   p = 0.4 p^2 = 0.16
2pq = 2 x 0.4 x 0.6 = 0.48 or 48 %

Therefore allele distribution is as follows:

RR (p^2) = 0.16(16%) Rr (2pq) = 0.48(48%) rr (q^2) = 0.36(36%)

Gene frequencies can change

Certain factors can act upon a genetic equilibrium and bring about significant changes to the frequency of some of the genes and change the composition of the gene pool. These factors include genetic drift, mutations and natural selection.

Sometimes variations in gene frequencies in populations occur by chance. This is known as random **genetic drift**. It may be an important evolutionary mechanism in small or isolated populations.

Say an allele occurs in 1% of the members of a species. In a large population, of say 1 000 000, then 10 000 individuals may be expected to possess the allele. By chance, the population of individuals with the allele will not be significantly altered in the next generation. If, however, the population is much smaller, say 1000 individuals, only one will carry the allele. By chance, this one may fail to mate and pass on the allele and so it will be lost from the population altogether.

An important case of genetic drift is when a few individuals become isolated from the rest of the species and start a new population, for example, when a few individuals colonise an isolated island or some new habitat.
These founder members of the new population are a small sample of the population from which they originated. By chance they may have a very different gene frequency. While the founder population remains small it may undergo genetic drift and become even more different from the large parental population. This process is called the **founder effect**. The effect undoubtedly contributed to the evolutionary divergence of Darwin's finches after strays from the South American mainland reached the remote Galapagos Islands.

Disasters such as earthquakes, floods, and fires may reduce the size of a population drastically. The result is that the genetic makeup of the surviving population is unlikely to be representative of the makeup of the original population. By chance certain alleles will be over represented among survivors, other alleles will be underrepresented, and some alleles will be eliminated completely. Because alleles for at least some loci are likely to be lost from the gene pool, the overall genetic variability in the population is usually reduced.

Evolution and Selection

Evolution is the process by which new species are formed from pre-existing ones over a period of time. The basis of contemporary thought surrounding the theory of evolution was first put forward by Alfred Wallace and Charles Darwin. In 1859 Darwin proposed natural selection as the force that causes changes in populations. More recently biologists have realised that natural selection can also maintain variation and therefore stabilise a population.

Natural selection

Charles Darwin (1809-1882) was employed as a naturalist and member of a scientific survey which sailed to South America and Australia in 1832. He visited a small group of volcanic islands called the Galapagos Islands. These are situated about 600 miles off the coast of Ecuador. When these islands were originally formed by volcanic activity no life existed there. Any plants or animals must have reached the islands by sea or air from the mainland. Darwin studied many different animals on the islands and was amazed by the variety of life-forms that existed there.

Darwin's observations of variation within a population and the tendency for the adult population to be stable in size led to the development of the idea of **natural selection**. The theory proposes that those organisms that are better adapted to their environment are more likely to survive and reproduce to produce offspring that are successful.

The theory is based on the following observations:
- In any population there is **variation.**
- Individuals within a population have the potential to produce large numbers of offspring yet the number of adults tends to stay the same from one generation to the next.

From these observations, two deductions were made:
- ✓ There is a struggle for survival (**competition**) with only the 'fittest' surviving.
- ✓ The individuals that survive and **reproduce** pass on to their offspring the characteristics that enable them to succeed (that is, a **selective advantage**).
- ✓ In time, a group of individuals that once belonged to the same species may give rise to two different groups that are sufficiently distinct to belong to two separate species.

If the environment or conditions change, then the features needed to survive in it will change, so natural selection is a continuous process.

During his voyage on *HMS Beagle*, Darwin found evidence of **adaptive radiation** in the **finch** population. He observed fourteen species, differing greatly but particularly in beak morphology, reflecting differences in feeding habits. It was suggested that soon after the Galapagos Islands formed they were populated by a flock of finches from the mainland. These then evolved by natural selection to fill the available vacant niches, as other perhaps better-adapted forms that would have been in competition with the finches had failed to reach the Islands.

- ❑ *Action*   List the different types of beaks found in finches.
                Describe how the beak shapes are adapted to different feeding niches.

There was no knowledge of genetics when Darwin put forward his theory of natural selection. The modern interpretation of the theory of evolution takes into account advances in modern genetics and refers to changes in the gene frequencies of a population. When environmental conditions change, there is a selection pressure on a species causing it to adapt to the new conditions. This pressure determines the spread of an allele within the gene pool. (see page(29) 'population genetics'.)

Darwin proposed natural selection as the force that causes changes within populations. More recently biologists have realised that natural selection can also maintain variation if there is no need to change and therefore stabilises a population.

Isolation and Speciation

Populations are groups of interbreeding individuals of the same species occupying the same habitat. In theory, any individual in a population is capable of breeding with any other. However, breeding sub-units may become separated in some way, that is, become isolated, and evolve along separate lines. If, reunited after many generations, the sub-units were found to be incapable of breeding successfully with each other, they would have become a separate species. Separation by geographical features, habitat changes, changes in body form and changes in breeding mechanisms may lead to the formation of new species.

Speciation

Within a population of one species there are groups of interbreeding individuals. Within each population there are breeding sub-units called **demes**. Individuals within a deme tend to breed with each other more often than they do with individuals of other demes. New species arise when some barrier to reproduction occurs so that the gene pool is divided and the flow of genes between separate demes may cease. Such a barrier which effectively prevents gene exchange between demes is called an isolating mechanism. If the separation is long-term, eventually the two groups will be so different that two new species incapable of interbreeding are formed. The separate species will each have their own gene pool. This process is called **speciation**.

Isolation leading to speciation

For new species to develop from a population, some form of isolating mechanism is required.

There are two main forms of **isolating mechanisms**:

- **Geographical isolation** between populations occurs when the population becomes physically split into separate demes. The physical barrier may be a mountain or a river or any feature which prevents the population of the same species from interbreeding. The evolution of a new species is very probable, given time. This sort of speciation is known as **allopatric speciation**.

Consider the isolation model where a population of birds with short flight range feed and breed only in the cool conditions of a valley and the lower slopes of two mountains a considerable distance apart. The birds are only able to breed at a certain temperature provided by the cool conditions. The mountain peaks are too cold for the birds to survive.

The climate then changes and it gets warmer. The birds tend to inhabit the nearest mountain and become confined to the cool mountain peaks. The birds are split into two separate breeding populations or demes, each with their own gene pool. Over a very prolonged period of isolation the birds may be subjected to different selection pressures. Because of the effect of natural selection on each gene pool the two populations may become sufficiently genetically different to prevent interbreeding. If the climate reverts to the original temperature and the birds are again able to inhabit the valley and lower mountain slopes they come into contact with each other. If the two populations have established a different gene pool and can no longer interbreed, then two separate species have evolved.

Darwin considered that species gradually change over long periods of time from one form to another. It would then be expected that biologists would find intermediate forms between one fossil species and the next in successive rock strata. However, these forms are surprisingly rare and this has led some biologists to believe that new species may arise relatively rapidly (perhaps within a few thousand years) and then remain unchanged for millions of years before changing again.

- **Reproductive isolation** within a population occurs when organisms inhabiting the same area become reproductively isolated into two groups when there are no physical barriers. Species formation occurring in demes in the same geographic area is known as **sympatric speciation**. The barriers to breeding include the following mechanisms:
  ✓ Behavioural isolation - in animals with elaborate courtship behaviour, the steps in the display of one subspecies fails to attract the necessary response in a potential partner of another subspecies.
  ✓ Mechanical isolation – the genitalia of the two groups may be incompatible.
  ✓ Gametic isolation – in flowering plants pollination may be prevented because the pollen grain fails to germinate on the stigma, whereas in animals sperm may fail to survive in the oviduct of the partner.
  ✓ Hybrid inviability – despite fertilisation taking place development of the embryo may not occur.

Hybrid sterility

One particular form of reproductive isolation is hybrid sterility. A hybrid may be defined as the offspring resulting from cross breeding of different species. When individuals of different species breed, the sets of chromosomes from each parent are different. These sets are unable to pair up during meiosis and so the offspring are unable to produce gametes. The hybrid is therefore sterile and the species is reproductively isolated. An example of hybrid sterility is a 'zebronkey'. This is the name given to the offspring which results from the mating of a zebra with a donkey. The zebronkey is sterile as it has 53 pairs of chromosomes that are unable to form homologous pairs at prophase I of meiosis.

5.6 Applications of reproduction and genetics

In the past, conventional breeding techniques have been used to improve farm animals, crop and ornamental plants. However, selection and cross breeding is laborious, time consuming and sometimes unpredictable. In the future the quality of farm animals may be improved by laboratory based breeding techniques involving embryos. Micropropagation provides a rapid method for obtaining large numbers of genetically identical plants.

Cloning

- A clone is an asexually reproduced, hence genetically identical, line of cells or organisms.
- Cloning can occur naturally, e.g. bacteria, yeast, plants grown from suckers, bulbs, corms.
- Artificial clones can be formed in animals by separating embryos at an early stage.
- Artificial clones can be formed in plants by taking cuttings and micropropagation.

Cloning of animals

Embryo cloning

This technique has been used to produce genetically identical individuals and has made it possible for farmers to increase the numbers of their animals. Eggs are taken from high milk yielding cows and are fertilised in a petri dish using sperm from the best bulls. This is known as in vitro fertilisation (commonly called 'test-tube fertilisation'). The fertilised egg divides to form a ball of cells. This group of cells or young embryo are split into separate cells. Each of these cells will then develop into a new embryo, genetically identical (clone) to the original. The embryos are then transplanted into other cows called surrogates.

This technique of embryo surgery has enabled farmers to increase their stock. This technique is also used to conserve rare breeds, where young embryos of young animals are bisected and successfully transplanted into a surrogate mother of a common breed to produce a new individual of the rare type.

Cloning by nuclear transplants

This technique allows clones to be produced from one individual. It involves transplanting a nucleus from a somatic cell into an egg cell. The following describes the procedure:
- ✓ Cells are taken from the tissues of the udder of a sheep (the donor) and cultured in a medium which stops division.
- ✓ An unfertilised egg is removed from a different sheep (the recipient) and the nucleus is removed leaving an egg cell without a nucleus.
- ✓ The donor and recipient cells are fused together and allowed to divide producing a ball of cells.
- ✓ The developing embryo is implanted into the uterus of another sheep (the host or surrogate).
- ✓ The lamb born is genetically identical to the original donor sheep.

This technique has enabled desirable qualities to be preserved for future generations. Embryo cloning allows many genetically identical copies of an animal to be produced. If a high milk yield mutation occurred in a cow, making her significantly better than other members of the herd, cross breeding with a bull would reshuffle her genes with a consequent loss of her unique characteristic. Cloning is the only technique that will conserve her unique features for future generations.

- The **advantages** of cloning in animals:
  - ✓ Cell culture is useful for production of cells in quantity e.g. cancer cells for medical research, monoclonal antibodies.
  - ✓ The production of a single, identical, genetic line of cells with desirable characteristics may be used to maintain genetic stocks.

- The **disadvantages** of cloning in animals:
  - ✓ In mammals the technique is very expensive and unreliable.
  - ✓ There may be the inadvertent selection of disadvantageous alleles.
  - ✓ Progeny may show long term/unforeseen effects such as premature aging.

Tissue culture

In theory, all cells can exist independently of the body provided they are supplied with the nutrients they require. Cells from young animals and cancer cells can be induced to divide in vitro. A few cells retain their ability to divide even in an adult. Examples are: new cells to heal wounds, to replace skin cells that have worn away, to produce new blood cells to replace worn-out ones and to replace cells in the digestive system to replace those that are constantly being worn away. Most cells, however, differentiate into cells which have specific functions, such as nerve or muscle cells, and most of these specialised cells do not normally divide again.

The technique of growing cells in a laboratory is called tissue culture. The medium, in which the cells are grown, has to be precisely controlled and conditions such as water potential and temperature have to be carefully monitored. Animal cells in tissue culture develop into mature cells of the same type as the cell from which the culture was started. Of course, all the cells are identical and contain identical genes to the parent cell.

Cell cultures have been used for some time for medical and research purposes, for example in the culture of viruses for vaccine production and also in the production of monoclonal antibodies. New techniques such as cell replacement therapy and tissue engineering are being developed.

Tissue engineering involves inducing living cells to grow on a framework of synthetic material to produce a tissue such as skin tissue. This has obvious applications for the treatment of extensive, deep burns. Normally when the skin is damaged, stem cells in the epidermis divide many times to form new skin cells that grow around and cover the wound. If the burns are deep the body is in danger of suffering fluid loss and infection. If the burns are not too extensive surgeons may take skin from other parts of the body and graft it onto the wound, but when large areas are burned this may not be possible. In 1998 an artificial skin called 'Apligraf' was approved and is now widely used in place of skin grafts.

Other applications of tissue engineering include blood vessel replacement, bone and cartilage repair, and the treatment of degenerative nerve diseases. Central to this area of research is the use of **stem cells**. A stem cell is an undifferentiated cell capable of dividing to give rise to cells which can develop into different types of specialized cells. Therefore, stem cells have the ability to develop and form all the tissues of the body. The best sources of these cells are from very early embryos, but some adult tissues, such as bone marrow, also contain stem cells. Therapeutic stem cell cloning has enormous medical potential. However, research with human embryonic cells is banned in some countries:

The technique may be described in simple terms as follows:
- ✓ A mature cell is taken from the patient and the nucleus is removed.
- ✓ The nucleus is removed from a human ovum.
- ✓ The mature cell nucleus is transferred into the 'empty' ovum.
- ✓ The ovum, containing the patient's DNA, divides to form a ball of stem cells.
- ✓ Stem cells are isolated and cultured with appropriate growth factors.
- ✓ Stem cells grow into the required organ or tissue.

In many cases of traditional tissue transplantation, the patient's immune system rejects the donated cells. This problem could be solved if the patient's own cells could be used to generate stem cells, then there would be no risk of rejection. Cloned stem cells could be used to generate organs for transplantation. This would prevent immune rejection and reduce the problem of organ shortages.

5.6 Applications of reproduction and genetics

The ethics of using stem cells

There is considerable controversy surrounding this area of research. The supply of embryos comes from the surplus embryos which were not placed into a female's uterus during fertility treatment. Once the stem cells are removed these embryos are then destroyed. Some think it is not acceptable to use embryos for this purpose even if there was never any chance of the embryo being allowed to develop. Others consider that the potential benefits outweigh the ethical concerns. The human stem cells could be used to treat Parkinson's disease, Alzheimer's disease, heart disease, liver diseases, diabetes, multiple sclerosis and some cancers.

Opponents also argue that embryonic stem cell technologies are a slippery slope to reproductive cloning and can fundamentally devalue human life. That is, there is the possibility to clone humans. Those in the pro-life movement argue that a human embryo is a human life and is therefore entitled to protection. Supporters of embryonic stem cell research argue that such research should be pursued because the resultant treatments could have significant medical potential. It is also noted that excess embryos created for in vitro fertilisation could be donated with consent and used for the research. The ensuing debate has prompted authorities around the world to seek regulatory frameworks and highlighted the fact that stem cell research represents a social and ethical challenge.

In vitro fertilisation (IVF)

In the last 25 years there has been a tremendous increase in the number of couples seeking help to conceive a child. A couple are described as infertile if they have failed to conceive after 12 months. A couple seeking fertility treatment will first be assessed to try to discover the cause of the problem. In the UK, 50% of the causes are the result of problems with the female's reproductive system, 35% are related to the male, and the rest cannot be explained. 50% of the females will eventually become pregnant whilst almost 60% of those with no obvious cause will achieve pregnancy, even without fertility treatment, within five years.

One form of treatment is called in vitro fertilisation or IVF. This technique involves mixing a female's egg or oocyte with the partner's sperm in a dish where fertilisation takes place.

Usually, ovulation is stimulated using hormones at a specific dosage which aims to cause several follicles to develop at the same time. The oocytes are collected from the female using a tube inserted through the vagina and into the oviducts. Ultrasound is used to guide the tube.

On the same day, the male's semen is collected and placed in liquid containing nutrients.

Each oocyte is placed in a separate dish and about 100,000 sperm are added to each. An alternate method involves injecting the sperm DNA into an oocyte.

Three days later the oocytes are examined to see which ones have been fertilised. Two are chosen and inserted into the uterus using a tube. Two are used to increase the chance that at least one will implant.

What happens to the 'unused' embryos has raised ethical issues. Some believe them to be human beings and should not be denied life. Others argue that females naturally lose embryos each month and that IVF embryos are no different. Others think that these embryos can be used as a source of stem cells, potentially a source of treatment for many genetic diseases. There is no world uniformity on the issue with some countries allowing this, while others have passed specific legislation to prevent it.

One possible use of the embryos following IVF is to freeze them using liquid nitrogen, allowing them to be stored for many years. A female may have to undergo radiotherapy or chemotherapy as part of her treatment for cancer and this may damage her ovaries. This raises another ethical issue. Before implantation of the stored embryos can be carried out permission of both partners is required. This can cause problems if the male partner no longer wants the woman to have his child.

Micropropagation

Plant tissue culture is known as micropropagation, the cloning of plants. Cells are taken from stock plants that have desirable characteristics and have commercial value. Conventional methods of plant propagation, such as taking cuttings, have been used for centuries. However, micropropagation has a number of advantages, notably the production of large numbers of plants that can be transported at an early stage of growth and so take up little space. The technique of micropropagation is based on the ability of the differentiated plant cell to give rise to all the different cells of the adult plant. That is, plant cells are **totipotent.** Micropropagation is sometimes referred to as a test-tube plant culture. It is an extremely cost effective way of producing large numbers of genetically identical plants which are clones of a single parent.

At the tip of the roots and shoots of plants are areas called meristems. Here the cells divide rapidly by mitosis, so the meristems are known as growing points. If cells are removed from the meristem and placed in suitable conditions, new, genetically identical, plants will develop.

These steps are generally followed in micropropagation:
1. A plant with the desired characteristics is selected.
2. A scalpel is used to remove the meristem from the shoot.
3. The meristem is cut into small pieces called explants.
4. The explants are placed onto a sterile, aerated nutrient medium, such as agar jelly.
5. The cells are allowed to divide by mitosis producing a mass of undifferentiated cells, called a callus.
6. The callus is subdivided and each piece is allowed to differentiate into a plantlet.
7. When they have reached a suitable size the plantlets are transplanted into sterile soil.

- *Action*   Rewrite the above steps in the form of a flowchart.

❖ The **advantages** of micropropagation are:

- Large numbers of plants can be grown in sterile controlled conditions ensuring a greater survival rate than would be the case if seeds were planted outside.
- Good quality stock are selected, possessing qualities such as resistance to disease or high yield.
- The crop is uniform since the plants are genetically identical. From a commercial viewpoint this is very important.
- Large numbers of plants can be stored in a small area with reduced heating and lighting costs.
- Unique genotypes can be preserved.
- Reduced space is required for transport.
- Only healthy stock are selected so plant diseases can be eliminated.

❖ The **disadvantages** of micropropagation are:

- Sterile conditions have to be maintained otherwise bacterial or fungal contamination of the culture medium may result with subsequent loss of plants.
- The plants are genetically unstable with an increased rate of mutation in medium-grown cells leading to abnormality in the plantlets. Regular inspection is needed to remove any defective individuals, thus labour costs are higher than with traditional propagation methods.

5.6 Human genome project

Human DNA consists of about 3000 million bases. The Human Genome Project began in 1990 involving scientists in many countries. It has been a mammoth task determining the order of bases in the human genome as well as the identification of genes, their sequencing and mapping. The identification of the 20,000 to 25,000 genes in human DNA took 13 years to complete. The next challenge is to assign functions to the identified genes.

Aims of the project

A genome is all the DNA in an organism, including its genes. Genes carry the information for making all the protein required by an organism. These proteins determine, amongst other things, the appearance of an organism, how it fights infection and perhaps even how it behaves.

The main aims of the project are to:
- determine the sequence of the four bases, A, T, G and C throughout all the human DNA.
- identify all the genes formed by the bases.
- find the location of the genes on the 23 human chromosomes.
- store this information on databases.
- consider all the ethical, social and legal issues which arise from obtaining information about the human genome.

Beneficial applications of the project

One of the main benefits of the project is that the information enables scientists to know exactly which sections of DNA, on which chromosomes, are responsible for the many different inherited diseases. In gene tests, scientists scan a patient's DNA sample for mutated sequences. A DNA sample can be obtained from any tissue, including blood. For some types of gene tests researchers design short pieces of DNA called probes the sequences of which are complementary to the mutated sequences. These probes will seek their complement among the three billion base pairs of an individual's genome. If the mutated sequence is present in the patient's genome, the probe will bind to it and flag the mutation. Another type of DNA testing involves comparing the sequence of DNA bases in a patient's gene to a normal version of the gene. Cost of testing can be very expensive and depends on the sizes of the genes and the numbers of mutations tested. The following are some of the main uses of genetic testing.

- carrier screening, which involves identifying unaffected individuals who carry one copy of a gene (recessive) for a disease that requires two copies for the disease to be expressed.

- pre-implantation genetic diagnosis

- pre-natal diagnostic testing

- newborn baby screening

- pre-symptomatic testing for predicting adult-onset disorders such as Huntington's disease

- pre-symptomatic testing for estimating the risk of developing adult-onset cancers and Alzheimer's disease

- Confirmation that an individual has a suspected disease

- forensic/identity testing

Some of the applications in more detail

- Once a sequence of bases is known it is possible to devise a reliable test to see if it is present. Using a sample of DNA from a person it is possible to identify whether that person is a carrier of a faulty gene such as that which causes cystic fibrosis. People who are carriers may decide not to have children or to have an antenatal genetic test to check if their child will be born with the disease. The incidence of some inherited diseases such as thalassaemia (an inherited blood anaemia disease common in some Mediterranean countries) is falling as a result of genetic testing.

- Some genes that have been identified play a contributory role in diseases later in life, such as Altzheimer's disease and breast cancer. Although genes play a part in disease development, so does the environment which includes people's diet and whether they smoke etc. Genetic testing can give an idea of the probability of developing a particular disease. Those people at greatest risk can then be targeted by health authorities, screened at regular intervals and given appropriate advice about how to reduce the risk by changing their lifestyle. The health trend is a move to prevention rather than cure. The former is far more cost-effective in the long term as well as being beneficial to the population as a whole.

- Once the base sequence of a gene is known it is then possible to find the protein that it codes for. Once the structure of that protein is known it is possible to design drugs whose molecules would fit it perfectly. It may be possible to design drugs that act against the gene itself.

- Knowing the base sequence of a normal, functioning gene makes it possible to eliminate all risk of the disease by correcting or replacing the faulty allele in humans.

What are the pros and cons of gene testing?

- Gene testing has already dramatically improved lives. Some tests are used to clarify a diagnosis and direct a physician toward appropriate treatments, while others allow families to avoid having children with devastating diseases or identify people at high risk for conditions that may be preventable. Aggressive monitoring for and removal of colon growths in those inheriting a gene for familial adenomatous polyposis, for example, has saved many lives. On the horizon is a gene test that will provide doctors with a simple diagnostic test for a common iron-storage disease (thalassaemia) transforming it from a usually fatal condition to a treatable one.

- Commercialized gene tests for adult-onset disorders such as Alzheimer's disease and some cancers are the subject of most of the debate over gene testing. These tests are targeted to healthy (presymptomatic) people who are identified as being at high risk because of a strong family medical history for the disorder. The tests give only a probability for developing the disorder. One of the most serious limitations of these susceptibility tests is the difficulty in interpreting a positive result because some people who carry a disease-associated mutation never develop the disease. Scientists believe that these mutations may work together with other unknown mutations or with environmental factors to cause disease.

- A limitation of all medical testing is the possibility for laboratory errors. These might be due to sample misidentification, contamination of the chemicals used for testing, or other factors.

- Many in the medical establishment feel that uncertainties surrounding test interpretation, the current lack of available medical options for these diseases, the tests' potential for provoking anxiety, and risks for discrimination and social stigmatization could outweigh the benefits of testing.

Social concerns

Who should have access to personal genetic information and how will it be used?
Who owns and controls the genetic information?
The public need to be educated in order to make informed choices.
The public need to be informed about the risks and limitations of genetic technology.
Should parents have the right to have their children tested for adult onset diseases?
Should a line be drawn between medical treatment and enhancement?
Is there a danger of one day producing human clones?

The following was reported in the April 2007 publication 'Nature Genetics'(Willard et al.)

Geneticists have now thrown several forms of DNA into human cells and created a long-desired prize: the first human artificial chromosome. "We put in three types of DNA and the chromosome self-assembled," says Huntington F. Willard of Case Western Reserve University School of Medicine in Cleveland, Ohio, USA.

The human artificial chromosome survived for as long as 6 months in cells, retaining its integrity while replicating during many cell divisions. Examining such synthetic chromosomes may provide scientists with a more accurate recipe for the elements of a natural human chromosome. That knowledge may then elucidate how, during cell division, a chromosome replicates and the resulting pair segregates to different cells.

Moreover, by placing genes onto artificial chromosomes and then inserting them into cells, investigators hope to study how a gene's chromosomal surroundings regulate its activity.

Gene therapy may also benefit from artificial chromosomes. Some researchers envisage a day when they can slip synthetic chromosomes containing genes that correct a disease into a person's cells.

Artificial chromosomes tantalize gene therapists, who face serious problems using viruses and other means to add genes to cells. Some viruses integrate genes into pre-existing chromosomes, which may cause mutations or affect the activity of the added gene. Other viruses shuttle genes into cells without integrating them, but the genes eventually disappear as the cells divide.

"In theory, an artificial chromosome would be a great advance because it wouldn't integrate but it would replicate and segregate," says Melissa A. Rosenfeld of the National Human Genome Research Institute in Bethesda, Maryland, USA.

Gene therapy

There are many diseases that are caused by faulty alleles of genes. The aim of gene therapy is to treat a genetic disease by replacing defective genes in the patient's body with copies of a new DNA sequence. Advances in gene technology and the success of the Human Genome Project in mapping the human chromosomes has enabled scientists to identify precisely many more genes responsible for genetic disease. About 60% of currently approved gene therapy procedures are targeting cancer with about 25% aiming to treat genetic disorders such as cystic fibrosis.

The main problem lies in developing a gene delivery system, that is, a means of inserting 'normal' versions of genes into a person's cells and ensuring that they function correctly once they get there. Gene therapy usually requires a vector or carrier to introduce the DNA. The majority of procedures use viruses as vectors to deliver the selected gene to the target cells. Some use liposomes and others use injection of naked plasma DNA.

There are two possible ways of replacing defective genes:

- Gene therapy involving **somatic cell therapy** targets cells in the affected tissues. This method may be therapeutic, but the genetic changes are not inherited.
  The use of stem cells, rather than mature somatic cells, is longer lasting in patients.
- **Germ-line therapy**, involves the introduction of corrective genes into germ-line cells, that is, the gene is replaced in the egg and will enable genetic corrections to be inherited.

Cystic fibrosis

Cystic fibrosis is due to a defective autosomal recessive allele. In the UK one person in 2000 suffers from the condition. Sufferers produce a thick sticky mucus from the epithelial cells lining certain passageways in the body. These secretions lead to a number of problems:

1. The pancreatic duct becomes blocked preventing pancreatic enzymes from reaching the duodenum and so food digestion is incomplete.
2. The bronchioles and alveoli of the lungs become clogged causing congestion and difficulty in breathing. The mucus is difficult to remove and leads to recurrent infections.

To relieve the distress with breathing, frequent daily chest physiotherapy massage is needed to keep the airways open. The sufferer also has impaired digestion and a limited absorption of food. Children with the condition have large appetites to try to compensate.

Cystic fibrosis is caused by a single defective recessive allele and therefore to inherit the disease both parents must be carriers of these alleles. Carriers can be identified using a simple blood test. The normal gene codes for the production of a protein found in the cell membrane. This protein, called cystic fibrosis transmembrane regulator (CFTR), transports chloride ions out of cells into mucus. Sodium ions follow out of the cells and water passes out of the cell by osmosis. This makes the mucus that lines the air passages a watery consistency. The protein of cystic fibrosis sufferers lacks just one amino acid and so cannot perform its transport function.

Microbiologists have succeeded in isolating and cloning the gene which codes for the CFTR protein. The gene therapy technique works as follows:

- ✓ The genes are inserted into liposomes (minute spheres of lipid molecules).
  This involves wrapping the gene in lipid molecules that can pass through the membranes of lung epithelial cells.
- ✓ An aerosol inhaler is used to add the non-defective gene to the epithelial cells of the lung.

✓ The liposomes fuse with the phospholipid bilayer of the cell membrane and the DNA enters the cells. These cells start to express the inserted gene by making the protein CFTR.

At the time of writing, trials have begun using this novel technique. The treatment does not solve the digestive problems of the patient but has the potential to solve the problem of congested and infected lungs.

Genetic counselling

If a family has a history of a genetic defect, unaffected members can consult a **genetic counsellor** for advice on the risk of bearing an affected child. Advice may be based on:
- Whether there is a history of the disorder in the family.
- Whether the parents are closely related.
- The frequency of the faulty gene in the general population.

Genetic screening
Once it is established that there is a risk of passing on a defective gene, there are means of investigating whether a child is affected before it is born. Techniques involved include:
- A blood test – there is a simple blood test for detecting cystic fibrosis.
- Amniocentesis – this involves withdrawing some of the amniotic fluid during the early stages of pregnancy. The fluid contains cells that have floated away from the surface of the embryo. These cells may be analysed microscopically.
- Chorionic villus sampling – early in pregnancy (within 8-10 weeks) tiny samples of foetal tissue are withdrawn from the uterus and cells are cultured and examined under the microscope.
  On the basis of these tests the parents can decide whether or not to have the pregnancy terminated.

Advantages and disadvantages of gene therapy

To find a defective gene scientists have to carry out the process of genetic screening. This genetic testing produces much controversy and raises many ethical and legal issues. Many believe that this involves an invasion of privacy. Some also believe that if prenatal tests are carried out, finding defective genes will lead to an increase in the number of abortions. Individuals with defects may be placed in a high risk group for insurance purposes to cover the cost of treatment. This would mean that insurance cover would be very expensive or even impossible to obtain.
Young couples may find that they are carriers of a genetic disease and must decide if they want to have a child that could be born with a defect.
Another problem involves the regulation of gene therapy in its use solely for reducing defects. Many fear that companies will use gene therapy for the wrong reasons, such as choosing or modifying the characteristics of a child.
The advantages of gene therapy far outweigh the disadvantages. To give a child that would be born with a genetic disease the chance of a normal life, or to prevent the development of cancer in an individual are goals that medical science must aspire to.

❏ **Action** Research the advantages and disadvantages of gene therapy.

Genetically engineered babies

The following was reported in the- 'Daily Mail' 2008

"Disease–free babies with three parents"

Babies genetically-engineered to be free from incurable diseases could be born in Britain within three years. Scientists at Newcastle University have already created ten embryos and are perfecting the controversial technique for use in IVF clinics. The aim is to prevent mothers from passing a range of incurable diseases, including some forms of diabetes, blindness and heart problems, to their unborn children. But critics say the technique - which involves creating embryos which effectively have three parents - defies nature and further erodes the sanctity of human life.

The research centres around mitochondria - sausage-shaped powerhouses inside cells which turn the food we eat into energy that can be used by the heart, muscles, brain and other parts of the body. Each mitochondrion has its own DNA which gives instructions on how to build and operate the powerpack and is passed down from mother to child. Defects in this DNA affect more than one in 5,000 babies and cause around 50 genetic diseases, some of which kill before adulthood. The scientists have found a way of swapping the damaged DNA with healthy genetic material, creating embryos free of mitochondrial disease. The "mitochondria transplant" begins by using IVF techniques to fertilise an egg. When the resulting embryo is still a few hours old the nucleus - which contains the genetic information from the mother and father - is removed and transferred into another woman's egg.

Researcher Professor Patrick Chinnery said: "We are trying to take away the diseased mitochondria and replace them with healthy ones, a bit like a transplant. We are swapping bad for good." The ten embryos made by the scientists each contain DNA from two women and one man. The embryos, which appeared healthy, were allowed to grow for up to six days before being destroyed which is a condition of the research licence.

Lead researcher Professor Doug Turnbull said the first babies could be born in three years. They would effectively have three parents - two mothers and a father. However, as mitochondria affect only the genetics of energy production, the children would look like their "real" parents and not the woman providing the healthy donor egg.

Current law says such embryos can be created for research but must be destroyed before they reach 14 days and cannot be implanted. An update of the fertility laws which is now before Parliament also bans such embryos from being used in IVF treatment. However, the ban could still be lifted before the Bill becomes law. Professor Chinnery said the technique had the power to transform lives. But critics accused the researchers of "meddling with the building blocks of life".

Josephine Quintavalle, of campaign group Comment on Reproductive Ethics said: "It looks like we have lost the plot in terms of any respect for the natural process." A spokesman for the Department of Health said the research was "promising" but the "safety aspects of implanting an embryo that has undergone a process of mitochondrial repair would need to be very carefully assessed". A charity at the forefront of genetics research is to increase its budget by 60 per cent to £4 billion over five years. The Wellcome Trust will expand investigations into the genetic basis of common diseases such as cancer, diabetes and psychiatric illness. The extra funding follows the "remarkable" performance of investments, it said. Trust director Dr Mark Walport said: "There are huge opportunities to advance medical research to improve health and wellbeing. "New technologies and approaches are revealing the causes of many major human diseases, providing new opportunities for prevention and treatment. This proposal will enable us to fund research aimed at tackling some of the world's major diseases."

The following was reported in the- 'Daily Mail' 2006.

"Ethical row over world's first 'made to order' embryos"

The world's first human embryo bank has been launched offering 'bespoke babies' for infertile couples. For around £5,000 couples can buy ready-made embryos matched to their specific requirements - even down to choosing what eye and hair colour they would like their child to have. In each case the embryos are made from eggs and sperm from two donors who have never even met. The moment of conception occurs in the laboratory and is determined by the genetic combination the clinic thinks will best meet the needs of the paying couples on its books.

Ethical campaigners last night condemned the move as the "absolute commercialisation of human life." They said it was heart-breaking that babies are now being treated as the equivalent of a supermarket "special offer". Currently in the UK,if one partner is infertile a couple can use donated sperm or eggs to create an embryo to be implanted in the woman's womb. Some couples can also use left-over embryos no longer needed by others who have undergone IVF. But the new service is totally different as it allows couples to buy fresh embryos that fit their requirements but which have no biological link to either of them. The human embryo bank is being run by The Abraham Center of Life in San Antonio in Texas. Although the clinic is in the USA, British women are expected to fly over for treatment. It boasts that its sperm donors all have doctorate degrees and most of its egg donors have college degrees, are under 25 and healthy. So far most of the couples on its waiting lists are happy just to get an embryo and have not set out detailed requirements.

However, some have asked for - and been allowed to join a list of recipients that will get - embryos made from blond haired and blue eyed donors. Whether a couple are put on the list for an existing embryo or one in the process of being created, they get 'portfolios' that include the donors' medical and social histories and usually a picture of them as a baby. To create the embryos the chosen donor is given drugs to make her produce eggs and once collected they are combined with the selected sperm. Out of a single cycle of eggs several couples - each paying $10,000 (£5,300) - will each get two embryos for implantation.

Centre director Jennalee Ryan said already she has a waiting list of clients for embryos and so as soon as they become available they are spoken for. She said unlike other embryo donation or adoption schemes, these are not left-over embryos from infertile couples. Because of the inherent problems that exist in such couples she said typically these only have a 30 per cent chance of producing a pregnancy. However she claimed the quality of the donor embryos she uses could offer double the chances of success. Ms Ryan said the idea of the bank came out of her existing adoption service when she realised that many couples would be keen to use donated embryos to create a family that way instead. She said babies given up for adoption tend to come from lower social groups and there is often a history of drug or alcohol abuse.

However, her egg and sperm donors are all well-educated and medically screened to ensure they have no health problems. She said it was also cheaper than adoption or IVF with an egg donor which in the USA can cost up to $20,000 (£10,500). "It offers an opportunity for couples to have a child who could not otherwise afford it," she said.

Ms Ryan admitted some people, especially religious groups, have objected to the bank. "But what I say to them is Jesus was not conceived in the normal way either. I don't lose any sleep over what we are doing. I feel what we are doing is positive. We are helping couples and putting good genes back into the universe." But Josephine Quintavalle of the UK campaigning group Comment on Reproductive Ethics said it amounted to the "absolute commercialisation of human life." She said: "It is heartbreaking to see children reduced in this way to the equivalent of a special offer supermarket commodity. Cut price, tailor-made human embryos, complete with door to door delivery." A spokeswoman for the Human Fertilisation and Embryology Authority said current rules would prevent any UK clinic from offering selection of embryos for non-medical reasons. But she confirmed there is no law to stop women from Britain going to the USA for such treatment.

- **Action** Do tabloid newspapers provide an accurate, scientific viewpoint?

Genetic engineering

Genetic engineering already has many commercial applications. Products such as insulin, enzymes and hormones can be produced on a large scale. In the near future it is hoped that the manipulation of genes will lead to the means to treat, or even cure, genetic disorders. There are, however, many concerns about the long-term effects of artificially altering DNA in organisms. These organisms are referred to as genetically modified organisms.

Uses of genetic engineering

- To transfer genes into bacteria, so that they can make useful products such as insulin.
- To transfer genes into plants and animals so that they acquire new characteristics, for example, resistance to disease.
- To transfer genes into humans so that they no longer suffer from genetic diseases such as cystic fibrosis.

Recombinant DNA technology

Genetic engineering involves the introduction of engineered DNA into cells in such a way that it will replicate and be passed on to progeny cells. One important application is the introduction of DNA from various organisms into bacterial cells, which then produce a required product. Recombinant DNA is formed when a piece of 'foreign' DNA is incorporated into the circular DNA (plasmid) from a bacterium. There are four stages in gene manipulation:

- The formation of DNA fragments including the gene required for replication.
- The splicing (insertion) of the DNA fragments into the vector.
- The introduction of the vector into the bacterium.
- The selection of the newly transformed organism for cultivation.

Key terms
> **Donor DNA** – a gene that is isolated for insertion.
> **Plasmids** – circular loops of DNA found in bacteria. The plasmid is known as a **vector.**
> **Restriction enzymes** – enzymes which cut DNA molecules between specific base sequences.
> **DNA ligases** – enzymes which join together portions of DNA.
> **Sticky ends** – the two ends of the 'foreign' DNA segment. They have a short row of unpaired bases that match the complementary bases at the two ends of the opened-up plasmid.
> **Recombinant DNA** – DNA which results from the combination of fragments from two different organisms.
> **Reverse transcriptases** – enzymes used to synthesize DNA from mRNA in specific cells.
> **Clone** – a population of genetically identical cells or organisms.

To explain the principles of using gene technology to produce useful molecules on a large scale, the production of **insulin** is described.

1.   Isolating the gene from a donor DNA molecule

Insulin is a small protein. The gene coding for insulin is located using a gene probe and then isolated from the rest of the DNA in a human cell. An enzyme called **restriction endonuclease** is used to cut the DNA into small pieces allowing individual genes to be isolated. The enzyme cuts DNA between specific base sequences which the enzyme recognises. Most restriction enzymes split the two strands in a staggered sequence. The unpaired bases at the cut form **sticky ends**.

2.   Inserting the gene into a vector

To get the gene into a bacterium a go-between or **vector** is used. The vector, in this instance, is a **plasmid**, a small, circular piece of DNA found in bacteria. In the case of insulin the bacteria used are called *E.coli.* To obtain the plasmids the bacteria containing them are treated to dissolve their cell walls and the plasmids are separated from the cell debris. The circular DNA molecule making up the plasmid is cut open using the same enzyme, **restriction endonuclease.**

The enzyme makes staggered cuts, called '**sticky ends**', that allow the donor DNA to be spliced into the vector DNA. This takes place when the donor and vector DNA are mixed together. The sticky ends are complementary and the C and G bases on their sticky ends pair up. Another group of enzymes, called **DNA ligases,** are used to join the donor and vector DNA together.
This created DNA is called **recombinant DNA**.

3.   Marker genes

Marker genes that confer antibiotic resistance are included in the recombinant DNA forming the plasmids. When the bacteria and plasmids are mixed together, only a small proportion of the bacteria take up the plasmids. If the bacteria are then cultured on a growth medium treated with antibiotic, only those containing the plasmid with the marker will survive.

Using the bacteria that have taken up a piece of foreign DNA successfully, the foreign DNA replicates along with the rest of the plasmid every time the bacterial cell divides. **Cloning,** of the recombinant containing bacteria, results in the production of multiple copies of the recombinant gene. That is, the bacteria divide repeatedly and give rise to a large population of bacterial cells all of which contain replicas of the foreign DNA.

4.   Manufacture and advantages

The genetically modified bacteria are cultured on a large scale using a **fermenter** and produce insulin which is extracted and purified. Thus, human insulin can be used instead of extracting insulin from animals. Also large quantities of product are produced quickly and relatively cheaply.

Doing it in reverse

Locating the correct piece of DNA is not easy as the cell contains two copies only of the DNA. However, the cell may contain large numbers of molecules of mRNA that has been transcribed from it. This is especially true if cells can be used which are known to synthesise and secrete the required product. The functional mRNA will be present in large quantities in the cytoplasm.
- This mRNA can be extracted.
- The addition of an enzyme made from viruses, **reverse transcriptase,** is used to make a DNA copy of the mRNA. This single strand of DNA is called copy DNA or cDNA. Many copies of cDNA are made.
- The addition of **DNA polymerase** converts this to a double strand for insertion into a plasmid as described above.

Genetically modified organisms

The main application of genetic engineering so far considered has involved health care.
✓ The production of human hormones, such as insulin and growth hormones.
✓ The production of antibiotics and vaccines.
✓ Gene therapy, where cells containing non-mutant genes are substituted for the abnormal mutant cells.

The production of insulin involved the introduction of human DNA into a bacterium. Since a transgenic organism is one that has had the DNA from another organism of another species transferred to it, the bacterium is a transgenic organism.

Human genes have also been transferred to animals. For example, a human gene that codes for an enzyme called antitrypsin used to treat cystic fibrosis, has been transferred to sheep which now produce milk containing this enzyme.

Genes have also been transferred into plants:
✓ The development of crop plants resistant to herbicides and pests, for example, by the transfer of genes that produce toxins with insecticidal properties from bacteria, to higher plants such as potatoes.
✓ Genes introduced into crops, such as tomatoes, to improve their flavour and extend their shelf life.
✓ Genes for tolerance to weed-killers introduced into soya bean plants.

Transgenic plants

A transgenic organism has had its genotype altered producing a new strain of organism. These are also known as genetically modified organisms.
Bacteria are readily introduced into plants. Certain species naturally attack damaged plants and cause the plant cells to multiply and form a tumour. The bacteria do this by inserting genes from their own plasmids into one of the plant's chromosomes. The plasmid gene links with the DNA of the plant but stimulates the growth of a tumour. Scientists can replace the tumour-forming genes in the bacterial plasmids with useful genes.
The following are examples of GM crops:
• Soya beans
In many countries soya beans are very important as a source of food. They are used as an ingredient in a wide range of foods such as flour, protein and oil. About 60% of food products such as bread, biscuits, baby foods, soya milk etc. are soya based. Certain varieties of soya plants have been modified to be tolerant to a weed-killer. This allows the weed-killer to be sprayed onto the crop without affecting it but kills all the weeds. The weed-killer breaks down in the soil into harmless components.
• Tomatoes
Tomatoes ripen naturally as they produce an enzyme which breaks down the pectin in their cell walls. Tomatoes sold at the supermarket need to be firm and at their best when displayed. This creates a problem for supermarkets that need to transport tomatoes long distances from their supplier. Scientists have developed a genetically modified tomato called 'Flavr Savr'. A gene has been introduced into the tomato plant that effectively blocks the production of the enzyme. The result is that Flavr Savr tomatoes have a longer shelf life and a better taste.

Benefits and concerns

A lay person may ask the following questions regarding GM foods. Are there potential risks in producing GM crops? Will the products and ingredients made from GM crops be labelled? Will the nutritional properties be affected? Will the environment be affected?

In theory on a world-wide scale GM crops have tremendous value:

- **Solving food shortages** in various parts of the world; perhaps also enabling crops to be grown in drought areas.
- **Producing improved food** with improved flavour and better keeping qualities.
- **Reducing the harmful effects of modern farming** by:
  - ✓ Introducing nitrogen-fixing genes into crops such as rice and wheat, reducing the use of artificial fertilizers.
  - ✓ Introducing genes that confer resistance to insects, weeds and diseases.

Since the introduction of GM crops at the end of the 20th century, there has been an increase in public concern and some scepticism regarding the research carried out by government agencies. As a result many retailers have banned GM ingredients from their own brand products. This will remain until public confidence in the long term use of GM crops is restored.

People are opposed to GM crops for the following reasons:

- How will the environment be affected?

There are concerns that the GM plants will transfer their genes to wild relatives or similar crops growing nearby with unforeseen effects. For example, plants with introduced genes that enable them to resist insect attack will quickly lead to the establishment of a resistant population of insect pests. Long-term field trials will establish whether these concerns are well founded.

- How safe is the food?

GM crops contain marker genes. These are short, easily detected sequences of DNA used to determine whether the organisms have taken up the introduced gene. Some marker genes confer antibiotic resistance. There is concern that these genes may be transferred to the bacteria in the intestine of the consumer.

- How will biodiversity be affected?

Plant breeding may fall into the hands of just a few commercial companies and the varieties they offer to the farmer will be reduced. This could make crops more susceptible to attack by pests and diseases and lead to a reduction in the use of important old varieties of their wild relatives.

- What effect will there be on the health of livestock?

Looking to the future, the real benefits from improved animal production might be seen in the Third World. For example, it may one day be possible to introduce disease resistance into otherwise vulnerable animals. There are well-advanced animal genome projects which parallel the successful mapping of the entire human genome. The Bovine Genome Project could result in, for instance, resistance to trypanosomiasis being introduced into more productive breeds of cattle from their naturally-resistant African counterparts.

Although there is no GM animal food on sale in supermarkets, farmers may be providing GM plants as a source of food to their animals.

- What will be the effect on organic farming?

If GM crops are to be grown commercially in the UK, organic farm produce will be compromised. Pollen from GM crops, spread on the wind and by insects, could find its way into organic fields and beehives. The distances required to prevent pollen transfer between crops are the subject of controversy and disagreement, although such measures have been commonplace in conventional seed production for many decades. Transfer is likely to occur, but given stringent separation distances some claim that it should be possible to limit the range and degree of any spread.

❑ ***Action*** Research the issues associated with GM crops.

GM Foods

The following conclusions regarding the growth of soya bean in Latin America were reported in an article by the 'Institute of Science in Society'.

"Soybean expansion in Latin America represents a recent and powerful threat to biodiversity in Brazil, Argentina, Paraguay and Bolivia. Transgenic soybeans are much more environmentally damaging than other crops because in addition to the effects from the production methods that involve heavy herbicide use and genetic pollution, they require massive transportation infrastructure projects (waterways, highways, railways, etc), which impact on ecosystems and make wide areas accessible to other environmentally unsound economic and extractive activities.

The production of herbicide resistant soybean leads to environmental problems such as deforestation, soil degradation, pesticide and genetic contamination, as well as socio-economic problems such as severe concentration of land and income, expulsion of rural populations to the Amazonian frontier and to urban areas, compounding the concentration of the poor in cities. Soybean expansion also diverts government funds otherwise usable in education, health, and alternative far more sustainable agro-ecological methods.

The multiple impacts of soybean expansion also reduce the food security potential of target countries. Much of the land previously devoted to grain, dairy products or fruits has been diverted to soybean for exports. As long as these countries continue to embrace neoliberal models of development and respond to demand from the globalized economy, the rapid proliferation of soybean will increase, and so will the associated ecological and social impacts".

The following was reported in Guardian newspaper (2008)

'GM soya 'miracle' turns sour in Argentina'

Seven years after GM soya was introduced to Argentina as an economic miracle for poor farmers, researchers claim it is causing an environmental crisis, damaging soil bacteria and allowing herbicide-resistant weeds to grow out of control.

Soya has become the cash crop for half of Argentina's arable land, more than 11m hectares (27m acres), most situated on fragile pampas lands on the vast plains. After Argentina's economic collapse, soya became a vital cash export providing cattle feed for Europe and elsewhere.

Now researchers fear that the heavy reliance on one crop may bring economic ruin.

The GM soya, grown and sold by Monsanto, is the company's great success story. Programmed to be resistant to Roundup, Monsanto's patented glyphosate herbicide, soya's production increased by 75% over five years to 2002 and yields increased by 173%, raising £3bn profits for farmers hard-hit financially.

However, a report in New Scientist magazine says that because of problems with the crops, farmers are now using twice as much herbicide as in conventional systems.

Soya is so successful it can be viewed as a weed itself: soya "volunteer" plants, from seed split during harvesting, appear in the wrong place and at the wrong time and need to be controlled with powerful herbicides since they are already resistant to glyphosate.

The control of rogue soya has led to a number of disasters for neighbouring small farmers who have lost their own crops and livestock to the drift of herbicide spray.

So keen have big farmers been to cash in on the soya bonanza that 150,000 small farmers have been driven off the land so that more soya can be grown. Production of many staples such as milk, rice, maize, potatoes and lentils has fallen.

Monsanto says the crop is the victim of its own success. Colin Merritt, Monsanto's biotechnology manager in Britain, said that any problems with GM soya were to do with the crop as a monoculture, not because it was GM. "If you grow any crop to the exclusion of any other you are bound to get problems. What would be sensible would be to grow soya in rotation with corn or some other crop so the ground and the environment have time to recover," he said.

One of the problems in Argentina is the rapid spread of weeds with natural resistance to Roundup. Such weeds, say opponents of GM, could develop into a generation of "superweeds" impossible to control. The chief of these is equisetum, known as marestail or horsetail, a plant which rapidly chokes fields of soya if not controlled.

But Mr Merritt said horsetail could be a troublesome weed in any crop. "I reject the notion that this is a superweed or that it will confer genetic resistance on other weeds and make them superweeds. It always has been a troublesome weed."

The soya was originally welcomed in Argentina partly because it helped to solve a problem of soil erosion on the pampas which had been caused by ploughing. Soya is planted by direct drilling into the soil.

Adolfo Boy, a member of the Grupo de Reflexion Rural, a group opposed to GM, said that the bacteria needed for breaking down vegetable matter so that the soil was fertilised were being wiped out by excessive use of Roundup. The soil was becoming inert, and so much so that dead weeds did not rot, he told New Scientist.

Sue Mayer, of Genewatch in the UK, said: "These problems have been becoming evident in Argentina for some time. It gives a lie to the claim that GM is good for farmers in developing countries.It shows it's an intensive form of agriculture that needs to be tightly controlled to prevent very undesirable environmental effects. It is not what small farmers in developing countries need."

Genetic fingerprinting

A person's DNA profile is known as their 'genetic fingerprint'. An individual's genetic fingerprint is unique, it is different to anyone else's. The technique of genetic fingerprinting can be used to provide forensic evidence and also determine parents in paternity cases. Since body cells contain the same DNA, tissues such as blood, hair, skin cells or semen can be used.

The technique of genetic fingerprinting

About 90% of the DNA of the human chromosome has no known function. Individuals acquire different sequences of this **non-functional DNA.** They vary in length but consist of sequences of bases, 20-40 bases long, often repeated many times. These unique lengths of non-coding DNA, known as hyper-variable regions (HVR) or short tandem repeats (STRs), are passed on to the offspring. It is the number of times that these lengths of non-coding DNA are repeated that is used to show the differences between individuals.

1. The DNA is extracted from the sample and cut into small fragments using restriction endonucleases.
2. The DNA fragments are separated by a technique known as electrophoresis. The fragments of DNA are placed at one end of a trough containing gel and exposed to an electric current. Since the fragments are negatively charged they move towards the positive terminal. The smaller the fragment the faster it moves and the DNA becomes separated into bands according to the size of the fragments.
3. The trough is covered with a nylon membrane and the fragments are transferred to the membrane by a process called Southern blotting.
4. Radioactive DNA probes (now largely replaced by non-radioactive or chemi-luminescent probes) are used to attach to specific parts of the fragments and any unbound fragments are washed off.
5. The nylon membrane with DNA fragments attached is placed under X-ray film and the radioactive probes expose the film.
6. This autoradiograph reveals a pattern of light and dark bands (the dark band indicates where a radioactive probe is present) which are unique to individuals and is called **a genetic fingerprint.**

The bands in a fingerprint are inherited from both parents: these can be used in paternity suits and can also be used to convict criminals. To do this, white blood cells are taken from the mother and the possible father. The bands of the mother are subtracted from the child's pattern. If the man is the true father, he must possess all the remaining bands in the child's genetic fingerprint.

Gene amplification using the polymerase chain reaction (PCR)

At a crime scene a small sample of DNA may be found, perhaps a single strand of hair or a small spot of blood. In order to carry out numerous laboratory tests larger samples are required. Using the PCR technique copies of specific fragments of DNA may be made. PCR rapidly produces many billions of molecules from a single DNA molecule. This enables tests to be carried out accurately and more rapidly regardless of the age of the sample.

PCR is really semi-conservative replication of DNA in a test-tube. The sample of DNA is dissolved in a buffer and mixed with the enzyme, DNA polymerase, nucleotides and short pieces of DNA called primers (which act as signals to the DNA polymerase to start copying).
The stages in the process are as follows:

1. The original DNA (target DNA) is denatured by heating to 95^0C and it separates into two single strands.
2. The solution is cooled to 55^0C triggering the primers to join to the complementary base

sequences on each of the single strands of DNA. This in turn triggers DNA replication.
3. The solution is heated to 70^0C and DNA polymerase (which is not denatured at this temperature) catalyses the synthesis of a complementary strand for each of the single strands of DNA, producing two identical double strands of DNA.
4. Steps 1-3 are repeated many times, doubling the quantity of DNA produced each time.

A genetic bank raises issues of privacy

Scientists are confronted with vast quantities of data, a large proportion of which is genetic fingerprinting information. This information is used for phylogenetic studies, forensic science, paternity studies etc. This raises concerns regarding the storage of this information as well as who has access to the data. Will insurance companies use the data to determine life and health insurance premiums?

On the wider issue of biodiversity of human beings, efforts are being made to store genetic material from the many races and tribes of the world before isolated tribes are intermixed and lost.This is scientifically useful, but careful ethical standards need to be maintained in order that genetic privacy is maintained and that no misuse of the information occurs in the future.

- *Action*   Research the issues raised by storing genetic data.

The advantages and disadvantages of genetic engineering

The advances made in genetic engineering have numerous advantages:
✓ The large scale production of complex proteins or peptides that cannot be made by other methods.
✓ The production of higher yielding crops with superior keeping qualities etc.
✓ The health benefits for treating genetic diseases.

There are also economic issues associated with the new techniques which are technically complicated and therefore very expensive on an industrial scale.

However, there are concerns that the development of genetic engineering will introduce the possibilities of misuse. There is no involvement of sex cells with gene therapy targeting body cells, so the cure is not inherited by the offspring. Far more controversial is germ-line gene therapy which involves replacing the defective gene or allele with healthy genes inside the fertilised egg. The offspring develops with the defective gene eliminated so that it will not be passed on to future generations.
This introduces the ethical question as to whether scientists have the right to alter the genotype of future generations. Do scientists know enough about how genes interact with each other? Some genes have no apparent function other than to control or 'switch off' other genes on the same chromosome. Tampering with genes in the fertilised egg could result in unforeseen effects in future generations.

There are a number of potential hazards associated with genetic engineering and it is impossible to predict what the consequences might be of releasing genetically engineered organisms into the environment. The potential hazards are:
✓ A new gene, on insertion, may disrupt normal gene function. For example, a potentially dangerous microorganism with a new gene may become a dangerous pathogen if it is released into the environment.
✓ Bacteria readily exchange genetic material. The recombinant DNA might get into other organisms. For example, herbicide resistance might be transferred to a weed species.
✓ The deliberate use of antibiotic resistant genes in *E. coli* ,which lives in the human gut, and the possibility that these genes could be accidentally transferred to human pathogens.
✓ The possibility of transfer of DNA with linked pathogenic genes, for example, oncogenes increasing cancer risks.

Obviously, scientists take precautions to minimise risk. Work on potentially dangerous pathogens has been restricted to isolated, highly specialised laboratories. However, despite legislation restricting the production and field testing of transgenic plants and animals there remains reservations about the long-term effects of the manipulation of the human genome and the production of GM modified organisms.

5.7 Ecosystems

Ecology is the study of how living organisms interact with each other and with their environment. An **ecosystem** is a natural unit of living (biotic) components in a given area, as well as the non-living (abiotic) factors with which they interact. An ecosystem is a major ecological unit. For example a forest consists of all the living organisms living there as well as the soil, rocks, water etc.

Components of an ecosystem

Ecology may be studied at a population, community, or ecosystem level.
- A **population** is a group of organisms of a single species occupying a particular area.
- A **community** comprises the different populations of species that live in a habitat.
- A **habitat** is the particular area occupied by a population. That is, the place where an organism lives. It has biotic and abiotic features which separate it from other habitats.
✓ the biotic features are the sum total of the organisms within the habitat and their interactions.
✓ abiotic features include different types:
- Edaphic features relate to the soil and include all its physical and chemical characteristics.
- Climatic features include light, temperature, moisture, salinity, and, particularly, the stability or variability of these.
- Microhabitats are small localities within a habitat, each with its own particular conditions.
- An ecological niche is the place of each species in an ecosystem. This is not only the physical space which it occupies but the role which it carries out within the community and its inter-relationships with other species as well. In the long term, two species cannot occupy the same niche in a specific habitat otherwise they compete with each other.

❏ *Action*   Give examples of ecosystems, habitats, populations and communities.

Nutrition

Nutrition is the process by which organisms obtain **energy** to maintain life functions and **matter** to create and maintain structure. These are obtained from nutrients.
Most **autotrophic** organisms use the simple organic materials, carbon dioxide and water, to manufacture energy - containing complex organic compounds, whereas **heterotrophic** organisms consume complex organic food material.

Energy flow through the ecosystem

The study of the flow of energy through the ecosystem is known as ecological energetics.
The energy from the sun enters the food chain at the producer level during photosynthesis and is the source of energy for the ecosystem.
The sun's energy is passed from one feeding or trophic level to another through the ecosystem. Energy is passed along a hierarchy of trophic levels with primary producers (plants) at the starting point of the chain. All animals are consumers. Primary consumers eat plants and are also called herbivores. Secondary consumers are carnivores, they feed on primary consumers. Tertiary consumers are carnivores that eat other consumers. Eventually the energy leaves the system as heat.
The following summarises the flow of energy through the ecosystem:
- Green plants trap solar energy and manufacture sugars from simple raw materials by the process of photosynthesis.
- Herbivores (primary consumers) are animals which feed on plants. Carnivores are animals that feed on other animals.
- Each of these groups forms a feeding or trophic level with energy passing from each level to a higher one as material is eaten.

- Only a small amount of the total energy that reaches the plant as light is incorporated into plant tissues. As energy is passed along the food chain there is a large loss at each level.
- At each level energy is lost through respiration, and through the excretion of waste products, so the amount of energy is reduced.
- The sequence from plant to herbivore to carnivore is a food chain and is the route by which energy passes between trophic levels.
- It is the loss of energy at each level which limits the length of a food chain so the number of links in a chain is normally limited to four or five.
- On the death of producers and consumers, some energy remains locked up in the organic compounds of which they are made. Detritivores and decomposers feed as saprobionts and contribute to the recycling of nutrients.
  - ✓ **Detritivores** are organisms which feed on small fragments of organic debris from plants and animals. This organic material is referred to as detritus and is made up of non-living organic material, such as faeces, fallen leaves and the remains of dead organisms. Examples of detritivores are earthworms and woodlice.
  - ✓ **Decomposers** are microbes, bacteria and fungi that obtain nutrients from dead organisms and faeces. They complete the process of decomposition started by detritivores.
  - ✓ **Saprobionts** include bacteria and fungi that feed by secreting enzymes on the food substrate absorbing the resulting products of this extracellular digestion.

Energy source

- The ultimate source of energy for ecosystems is the sun from which energy is released in the form of electromagnetic waves.
- A good deal of the solar energy reaching the Earth's atmosphere does not penetrate it. It is reflected or absorbed and radiated back into space by the ozone layer, dust particles and clouds.
- Also about 90% of the energy reaching the surface of the Earth is reflected by vegetation, soil, and water or absorbed and radiated to the Earth's atmosphere as heat.
- This means that only about 10% is left for producers to make use of. Therefore, only a small part of the total amount of energy reaching the Earth's atmosphere enters ecosystems. Also, the quantity absorbed by plants varies considerably at different latitudes.
- Of the energy entering a plant only 1% to 5% is utilised by the plant, the rest is lost, partly by reflection and partly by the evaporation of water.

Trophic efficiency

- This is the percentage of energy at one trophic level which is incorporated into the next trophic level. The rate at which energy passes into the animals at each trophic level is about 10% of that entering the previous level. This is called the **gross ecological efficiency**. This value differs from one ecosystem to another with some of the highest values, around 40%, occurring in oceanic food chains. Some of the lowest values, around 1%, are found in ecosystems where most of the animals are birds or mammals.

Example:
- In a particular food chain, if 15000kJ of energy enters the primary consumer level and 1500kJ passes to the secondary consumer level, then:

Gross ecological efficiency =

$$\frac{15000}{1500} \times 100 = 10\%$$

Energy flow

Energy flow through producers

The energy flowing from one organism to another in the food chain originates as sunlight.
A large proportion of the energy that falls on a plant is not absorbed:
If it is assumed that 100 units of energy per unit time reach the leaves of a crop plant:

Units of energy	What happens to the energy?
50	The 'wrong' wavelength, that is, the photosynthetic pigments absorb mainly light at the red and blue parts of the spectrum.
10	Some of the light is reflected and some passes straight through the leaf, that is, it is transmitted.
30.8	Lost in the processes of photosynthesis and evaporation.
9.2	Incorporated into plant products such as glucose
3.7	Used up in the process of respiration.

Photosynthetic efficiency indicates the ability of a plant to trap light energy.

= <u>Quantity of energy incorporated into product</u>
Quantity of energy falling on the plant

This is normally less than 10% and depends on external factors such as light intensity and temperature.

- **Gross primary productivity** (GPP) is the rate at which products, such as glucose, are formed.

- A substantial amount of gross production is used up in respiration by the plant.
Using the figures in the above table:

GPP minus respiration = net production.
9.2 – 3.7 = 5.5 units.

That which is left over after respiration is called **net primary productivity** (NPP). This represents the food available to primary consumers. In crop plants this represents the yield which may be harvested.

- **Secondary productivity** is the rate at which consumers accumulate energy in the form of cells or tissues.

Biological productivity is the rate at which biomass accumulates in an ecosystem.
Biomass is the dry weight of organic matter comprising a group of organisms in a particular habitat.

Biological productivity has two components:
1. Primary productivity – the production of new organic matter by green plants.
2. Secondary productivity - the production of new organic matter by consumers.

Energy flow through consumers

Consumers have a conversion efficiency of about 10%, that is, for every 100 grams of plant material taken in or ingested, only about 10 grams is incorporated into herbivore biomass. This means that only part of the NPP of the ecosystem is transferred to the primary consumers.

Herbivores are not able to eat all the vegetation available to them.

Consider a cow feeding on grass in a field.

- ✓ Some of the plant material is not eaten by the cow. Cattle grazing a field will eat the grasses and edible weeds but do not eat the roots and often leave the woody parts of the plants.
- ✓ Cows feed on plant material which contains cellulose which they are unable to digest. This passes out of the body as faeces containing a high proportion of undigested matter. (In terms of the ecosystem this energy is not wasted as it is available to decomposers).
- ✓ Some of the food material in the field is being eaten by other herbivores, such as rabbits.

Much of the energy in the food consumed by a cow is lost mainly by two processes:
- ✓ Respiration - about 30% lost as heat
- ✓ Excretion - about 60% lost in urine and faeces.

Farmers increase the productivity of their livestock by keeping the animals in barns during the winter months. Why?

Herbivores have a lower secondary productivity than carnivores. That is, carnivores are more efficient at energy conversion than herbivores. They have a much higher secondary productivity. This is because their protein-rich diet is more readily and efficiently digested. Only about 20% of the energy intake is lost in the faeces and urine of carnivores compared with a loss of about 60% in herbivores.

Carnivores absorb almost twice as much energy per unit mass of food compared with herbivores.

The loss of energy at each trophic level gives ecological pyramids their characteristic shape.

Pyramids of energy

The number of organisms, their biomass or the amount of energy contained in each trophic level can be represented in diagrams with a bar for each level. These are known as pyramids. They provide a quantitative account of the feeding relationships in a community. The most accurate way to represent the feeding relationships in a community is to use a **pyramid of energy**.

A pyramid of energy shows the quantity of energy transferred from one trophic level to the next, per unit area or volume, per unit time. This represents the total **energy** requirement of each successive trophic level in a food chain. As material passes up through the food chain energy is lost in respiration as heat, and in excretion, so the size of the bars decreases sharply. Since only some of the energy is passed on from one level to the next, energy pyramids are never inverted as in biomass pyramids.

The use of a set period of time means that an energy pyramid overcomes the problems which arise when ecosystems are compared simply by counting or measuring the standing crop of organisms.

Pyramids of energy enable ease of comparison of the efficiency of energy transfer to be made from one trophic level to the next between different communities.

However, obtaining the data can be complex and difficult.

Succession

Community and succession

The distribution of species does not necessarily remain the same over long periods of time. Ecosystems are dynamic and subject to change. Organisms and their environment interact, if one changes so does the other. A change in the environment affects the organisms, and a change in the organisms affect the environment.

An area of bare ground does not remain free of vegetation for long as any gardener knows! Weeds are usually the first plants to grow, followed by grasses then taller plants. Provided the soil conditions are suitable, over a very long period of time the bare ground would eventually become woodland. Succession is the change in structure and composition of species over time.

- **Primary succession** refers to the introduction of plants/animals into areas that have not previously supported a community, for example, bare rock, or the site of volcanic eruption.
- **Secondary succession** refers to the reintroduction of organisms into a bare habitat previously occupied by plants and animals. If the original vegetation is removed, for example by fire, or by tree felling, the area rapidly becomes re-colonised by a succession of different plants and animals.

In any area, over time, new organisms replace existing ones, that is, species diversity increases until a stable state is reached. All successions usually involve changes in community structure and function until a community reaches a climax of succession known as the **climax community**, for example, a mature woodland. This is a stable community which undergoes no further change.
The different stages in a succession are known as **seres**.

Consider the colonisation of bare rock.
The first organisms to colonise the bare rock are **algae** and **lichens.** These plants are called pioneer species and form a **pioneer community**. Lichens slowly erode the rock. This together with the weathering of the rock and the accumulation of dead and decomposing organic material leads to the formation of a primitive soil. Wind blown spores allow **mosses** to appear and as the soil develops **grasses** become established. As the soil builds up deep-rooted **shrubs** appear. Over a very long time **trees,** such as oak, become established. This is then known as the climax community. This is a stable condition dominated by long-lived plants.

It should be noted that a community consists of animals as well as plants and that the animals have undergone a similar succession dictated by the plant types present at each stage.
In a secondary succession, seeds, spores and organs of vegetative reproduction may remain in the soil and dispersal of plants and migration of animals will assist in colonisation of the habitat.

Human interference can affect a succession and may prevent the natural development of the climax community:
- ✓ Grazing by sheep.
- ✓ Heather moorland management by controlled burning for grouse shooting.
- ✓ Farming of land.
- ✓ Deforestation and soil erosion.

5.8 Effects of human activities

The process of evolution is normally slow but the effect of human influence on the environment has created new selection pressures. Examples are warfarin resistance in rats, and resistance to antibiotics in bacteria. Organisms are said to be resistant to a chemical poison if they are able to survive exposure to a dose of that poison which would normally be lethal to it.

Resistance in rats

The pesticide 'warfarin', which is an anticoagulant, has been used on a large scale to control the rat (*Rattus norvegicus)* population. Rats have become resistant to warfarin.
A dominant allele R at a single locus in rats confers resistance. However, this allele also confers a requirement for vitamin K.

✓ Heterozygotes (Rr) are resistant to warfarin and have only a small requirement for vitamin K.
✓ Homozygotes (RR) are resistant to warfarin but have a massive requirement for vitamin K which is difficult to meet.
✓ Homozygotes (rr) are killed by warfarin but have a much better chance of survival than RR rats if warfarin is absent from the environment.

This is an example of **heterozygote advantage** where the heterozygotes are favoured by selection and both alleles Rr will be maintained in the population with all three genotypes RR, Rr and rr being produced in each generation. In the rat population both warfarin sensitive and warfarin resistant alleles are maintained in areas where warfarin is used as a selective agent.

Antibiotic resistance

The use of antibiotics to treat disease in the human population has had obvious benefits. However, in agriculture many farm animals are reared indoors so that they grow more rapidly. For example poultry kept in confined areas. In these crowded conditions there is a greater risk of disease spreading, therefore broad-spectrum antibiotics are often added to animal food in an attempt to prevent disease. Although the prophylactic use of small quantities of antibiotics in animal feed has led to healthier, faster growing animals, this widespread increased use of antibiotics has led to the development of resistance among many species of bacteria.

Many bacteria that were previously susceptible to antibiotics have now become resistant. Resistance to a chemical poison is the ability of an organism to survive exposure to a dose of that poison which would normally be lethal to it. This resistance has arisen because of random mutations. Mutations are rare but as bacteria multiply rapidly, one every 20 minutes under optimum conditions, there is a greater chance of mutations occurring. Most gene mutations are recessive and rarely expressed in combination with a dominant gene. However, repeated exposure to antibiotics has led to more bacteria surviving and passing on resistant genes.

- In the past antibiotics have perhaps been prescribed too readily by many doctors in general practice (GP's). Reducing the number of antibiotics in use means that fewer bacteria are exposed to them and reduces the chance of resistant strains appearing.
- Resistance arises by mutations occurring randomly within populations of organisms which then confers an advantage in the presence of that antibiotic. This may be the ability to produce an enzyme which breaks down the antibiotic. For example, some bacteria have developed an enzyme, penicillinase, which renders penicillin ineffective. In the presence of penicillin non-resistant forms are destroyed. There is a selection pressure favouring the resistant types. The greater the quantity and frequency of penicillin use, the greater the selection pressure.

- The problem has been made worse by the discovery that resistance can be transmitted between individuals of the same species. There is evidence that the resistance may be passed from one organism to another on plasmids, during conjugation (sexual reproduction). This means that a disease-causing organism can become resistant to a given antibiotic even before the antibiotic is used against them.
- MRSA (methycillin resistant *Staphylococcus aureus*) has developed a resistance to several antibiotics. Antibiotics are widely used in hospitals, especially to prevent infections occurring from surgery. This organism originated in Australia and within ten years has spread world-wide. A sample of *Pseudomonas aeruginosa* has been identified as being resistant to all clinical antibiotics. Such organisms are becoming a more common problem and the antibiotics available to treat them are becoming very limited in number.

Artificial selection

Humans have selectively bred plants and animals for thousands of years. This artificial selection is accomplished by the selection and mating of animals and plants that show desirable characteristics. Techniques such as artificial insemination and embryo transplantation have increased the success of selective breeding in animals.

Artificial selection

Artificial selection or selective breeding of animals and plants makes use of variations that occur within a population. Humans choose organisms showing desirable characters and breed only from these. In terms of genetics, humans rather than the environment determine which alleles are passed on to future generations and which are lost. This process of artificial selection mimics natural selection and provides evidence that selection can lead to the development of characteristics and the production of very distinct forms of organisms, as seen in many domestic animals and plant species.

Artificial selection :
✓   is carried out by humans to obtain plants or animals with the characteristics humans require.
✓   may take many years to develop organisms with the required characteristics.
✓   produces organisms belonging to the same species, but are often described as different breeds or varieties.

There are two basic methods of artificial selection:
•   **inbreeding** – occurs when the gametes of close relatives fuse.
The problem with inbreeding is that it promotes homozygosity. That is, it increases the chance of a harmful recessive gene expressing itself, since there is a greater risk of a double recessive individual occurring. For example, plant species inbred over many generations show a degree of loss of vigour, size and fertility. This is called inbreeding depression. At intervals it is necessary to introduce new genes by outbreeding.

•   **outbreeding** – occurs by the crossing of unrelated varieties.
Outbreeding promotes heterozygosity. It introduces hybrid vigour where the organisms sometimes grow more strongly. It arises when the new sets of chromosomes are complementary in their effects. Occasionally crosses have occurred between plants of different species e.g. the development of modern wheat.

There are five main steps in any **breeding programme**:
1.   Look for individuals with the characteristics you require, e.g. resistance to disease.
2.   Breed together two of these individuals (or self-pollinate if it is a plant).
3.   Collect the offspring, and select those which have the characteristics you require.
4.   Breed from these offspring.
5.   Repeat these steps over many generations.

An example of selective breeding in animals is milk yield in cattle.
To develop cows with an increased milk yield the following steps would be carried out:
1.   Test the milk yield of selected high milk yielding cows;
2.   select the cow with the highest milk yield (A);
3.   select a bull descended from a cow with a high milk yield (B);
4.   cross cow A and bull B, and select female calves;
5.   wait for these calves to mature, then test their milk yield;
6.   select the cow with the highest milk yield (C), then repeat these steps over several generations.

Endangered species

Bio-diversity and extinction

Human activities are altering ecosystems upon which they and other species depend. In the oceans stocks of many fishes are being depleted by over-harvesting, and some of the most productive and diverse areas, such as coral reefs and estuaries are being severely stressed. Globally, the rate of species loss may be as much as fifty times higher than at any time in the past 100,000 years. Extinction is a natural process that has been taking place since life first evolved. It is the current *rate* of extinction that underlies the bio-diversity crisis. Scientists believe that the normal 'background' rate of extinction is one out of every million species per year. It is now estimated that human activity in tropical areas alone has increased extinction rates between 1000 and 10,000 times! Massive destruction of habitats throughout the world has been brought about by agriculture, urban development, forestry, mining, and environmental pollution. Marine life has also been affected. About one third of the planet's marine fish species rely on coral reefs. At the current rate of destruction about half of the reefs could be lost in the next 20 years.

Endangered species

The vast majority of Earth's earlier occupants, including the large and once dominant dinosaurs and tree ferns, have become extinct largely as a result of climatic, geological and biotic changes. At the present time, human activity has taken over as the main cause of species extinction. Many of the larger mammals such as mountain gorillas, giant pandas, tigers and polar bears are threatened.
Their decline in numbers has three main causes:

- loss of habitat
- over-hunting by humans
- competition from introduced species.

Other species are also threatened by additional causes such as:
- deforestation
- pollution
- drainage of wetlands.

It is now recognised that each species may represent an important human asset, a potential source of food, useful chemicals, or disease-resistant genes. There is therefore a need for **species conservation**, the planned preservation of wildlife.

Conservation of genetic sources

The conservation of species ensures the conservation of existing gene pools.
For ethical reasons it is important to conserve potentially useful genes for future generations of humans as well as for the survival of the species itself.

Present-day plants and animals used in agriculture and horticulture have been developed from plants and animals that were originally in the wild. Breeding increases genetic uniformity with the loss of rarer alleles. In the past breeders may have neglected some important qualities, such as resistance to cold and disease etc. These need to be added back into highly cultivated varieties, using the wild plants and animals as a gene bank. If habitats, and the wildlife that live in them are threatened, this may no longer be possible. There is also concern about the progressive destruction of the tropical rain forests.

Among the many trees and shrubs are some with medicinal properties. The extinction of any plant species before its chemical properties have been investigated could amount to an incalculable loss. In recent years there has been much concern about the loss of gene pools and legislation has endeavoured to prevent the extinction of endangered species.

The following are some of the steps that have been taken:
- Stocks of seeds of 'traditional' varieties of plants are stored in seed banks.
- The establishment of sperm banks.
- The founding of rare breeds societies to maintain old, less commercial varieties of animals.
- The protection and breeding of endangered species in specialised zoos.
- Reintroduction programmes, e.g. Red Kite in mid Wales.
- Global organisations, such as the World-Wide Fund for Nature, mount continuing campaigns to promote public awareness.
- International co-operation restricting trade, e.g. in ivory and whaling.
- In the UK, the Nature Conservancy Council is the government body that promotes nature conservation. It gives advice to government and to all those whose activities affect wildlife and their habitats.
- ✓ It produces a range of publications.
- ✓ It proposes schemes of management for each of the major ecosystem types, endeavouring to conserve species diversity.
- ✓ It establishes nature reserves managed by wardens.

Education and legislation have also played their part in conservation.
Legislation has been introduced to protect endangered species and to prevent over-grazing, over-fishing, hunting of game, collection of birds' eggs, picking of wild flowers, and plant collecting.

Agricultural exploitation

Humans are dependent on the Earth's resources for their survival. The increase in human population has meant that more food has to be produced to support it. In agriculture an increase in land use and over-fishing of the oceans has led to a conflict between production and conservation. The use of pesticides and fertilizers have improved crop yield but environmental issues arise from their use.

Agricultural exploitation

Conflicts can sometimes exist between farming and conservation.

The main purpose of agriculture is to produce food for human consumption. Both the efficiency and the intensity of food production are being continually increased to meet the demands of the human population. This was particularly evident in the years following World War II when the government encouraged farmers to obtain the maximum possible yield from the land. More land was cultivated, the use of fertilizers and pesticides was increased, mechanisation was introduced.

These changes had a number of environmental implications:

- To make **larger fields** many **hedgerows were removed**. The larger machinery that was needed to prepare the soil and harvest crops could be used more efficiently in larger fields and land previously covered by hedges could now be used for growing crops.
- In the larger fields single crops were grown, for example wheat and barley. This is called monoculture and is the simultaneous growth of large numbers of crop plants of similar age and type within a defined area. Monoculture is an 'artificial' situation because there will normally be a succession leading to a greater diversity of species. If the same crop is grown on the same plot year after year, yield progressively declines. This is due in part to mineral depletion but also because conditions become ideal for the crop plant's pests and parasites. This is resisted in monoculture by the use of selective **herbicides** to prevent the growth of weeds, and **pesticides** to remove insect and other pests.
- The maximum use made of available agricultural land by intensive cultivation necessitated a huge increase in the use of inorganic fertilizers which had unforeseen environmental effects, such as eutrophication of waterways.

In recent years the views of government, farmers and consumers have changed. People are far more aware of the value of the countryside not only because it is a source of food but also because it provides a habitat for plants and animals as well as a place to visit for relaxation and enjoyment. Schemes are in place to encourage farmers to manage their farms for biodiversity. Some land is given over to conservation and the farmers receive a grant to compensate them for reduced income. Since the Environment Act was passed in 1995 the loss of hedgerows has been reversed. Hedges are important as they provide habitats for insects and birds that live and feed on them. They also provide nesting sites for birds. Hedges act as wildlife corridors enabling birds and mammals to move from one area of woodland to another, helping to maintain the biodiversity of the woodlands.

Deforestation

Forests cover about 34% of the world's land surface. However, about half the world's forests have been cut down by deforestation during the last 30 years. The sale of valuable timber, the freeing of land for alternative uses such as subsistence farming and cash crops, clearing land for roads etc, has meant that the trees of forests and woodland are being cut down faster than they can be replanted or regenerated naturally. Forests help to maintain a balance of carbon dioxide and oxygen in the atmosphere.

Reasons for deforestation:
- ✓ There is a world demand for timber as a building material.
- ✓ Wood is used as a fuel.
- ✓ Land is cleared for farming.
- ✓ New roads are built to provide a transport infra-structure.
- ✓ There is a demand for paper and packaging.

Consequences of deforestation:

- **Climate change**

The rate at which carbon dioxide is removed from the atmosphere by the process of photosynthesis is being reduced by cutting down forests. On a global scale this is a massive reduction and contributes to global warming.

- **Destruction of natural habitats**, leading to a reduction in biodiversity. It is estimated that at least 50% of the Earth's species live in the tropical rain forests, even though they only occupy about 10% of the Earth's land area. If natural habitats are destroyed this may lead to the loss of medicinal properties of some tropical plants that may become extinct before their clinical properties have been investigated.

- **Soil erosion**

- ✓ Digging and ploughing loosens the topsoil, assisting in the process of soil erosion.
- ✓ The removal of vegetation affects regional climate mainly by reducing rainfall thus accelerating desertification.
- ✓ Deforestation of the watershed causes lowland **flooding**.

  The removal of vegetation on the higher slopes of valleys results in heavy rain sweeping exposed soil to the flood plains below. On the lower slopes, plants and leaf litter would normally act as a sponge soaking up heavy rainfall, and water would gradually be released into the soil. Instead, due to the absence of plants, only evaporation occurs. This is generally slower than transpiration in returning water vapour to the atmosphere, so soil conditions become wetter.

Forest management

Woodland and forests have been used as a source of timber for thousands of years. With careful management, it is possible to make use of this resource without destroying the ecosystem. However, maintaining a sustainable forest ecosystem while timber is being removed on a large scale is extremely difficult. In certain areas there is a tendency to clear an area and then move on, leaving the area devoid of vegetation leading to soil erosion. With careful management it is possible to take the steps necessary to minimise damage to the ecosystem.

Managed forestry involves sustainable replanting and regeneration.

- In Britain the technique of **coppicing** has been used for thousands of years. This traditional woodland management system is based on the fact that most deciduous trees grow from the base when their trunks are cut down. The trees are cut down close to the ground and then left for several years to re-grow. The new growth consists of a number of shoots and the wood harvested can be used for making small items of furniture or fencing.

- Instead of removing all the trees in an area at one time, **selective cutting** can be used. This involves felling only some of the largest trees, leaving the others in place. This can be difficult in practice since the large machinery used to fell and drag out the trees cause considerable disturbance to the area. Selective cutting is valuable on steep slopes where the total removal of trees would leave the soil very vulnerable to erosion. Selective cutting also helps to maintain nutrients in the forest soil, reduces the nutrient loss, and minimises the amount of soil that is washed into nearby waterways.

- **Long rotation time** also increases sustainability. This involves leaving each part of the forest for many years before re-harvesting it. Again this is difficult in practice in some parts of the world. In Britain traditional forestry would have left trees to grow for up to 100 years. In some modern forestry industries, such as those which provide wood for paper, the trees are allowed to grow for only 10 years before harvesting. Short rotations like this do not allow time for species diversity to build up. Also the frequent disturbance by machinery can cause damage to the soil.

With good forestry practice efficiency can be increased in several ways:
- ✓ Planting trees the optimum distance apart.
  Planting trees too close together will result in intra-specific competition. This results in the trees growing tall and thin producing poor quality timber.
- ✓ Controlling pests and diseases.
  If trees grow well, this results in a high quality harvest of timber. This means that fewer trees need to be felled. Best use is made of the land, reducing the total area of land required.

If timber is cut from a forest in such a way that a similar number of trees are removed year after year for long periods of time, the forest ecosystem can be maintained. This means that the habitats are left intact and species are able to live in the forest even though timber is being extracted.

In Europe it is important to preserve native woodlands and to provide **protected areas** to preserve species. Efforts are also being made to conserve the dwindling areas of tropical rain forests. This involves the development of habitats which are legally safeguarded and patrolled by wardens. This gives authorities greater powers to control developments and activities within designated areas.

Another important development is that of 'ecotourism'. That is the responsible travel to natural areas that conserves the environment and improves the well being of local people.

Ideally, ecotourism should:

- ✓ Minimize the negative impacts of tourism.

- ✓ Contribute to conservation efforts.

- ✓ Employ local people and give money back to the community.

- ✓ Educate visitors about the local environment and culture.

- ✓ Cooperate with local people to manage natural areas.

- ✓ Provide a positive experience for both visitor and host.

Native woodlands

In 1919 the Forestry Commission was set up to establish a national forestry reserve. Since then vast areas of non-native conifers have been planted. These have been planted rather than native trees as conifers produce more timber in a shorter time and can also grow on infertile soils. At present woodland covers 10% of the UK but of this area only 1% consists of natural or native woodland. It is essential that these native woodlands are preserved in order to maintain and enhance biodiversity. There is a need to plant more native species to provide a wide range of habitats for the great variety of species that live there.

Overfishing

Pressure on global fish stocks is certain to intensify as human numbers rise and wealth increases, and the few marine wild fisheries which are not yet completely exploited will inevitably face growing pressure. Global demand for fish has doubled in under 30 years, because of population growth in poor countries and a matching increase in demand for fish there. In addition to the hundreds of trawlers and small fishing boats there has been a large increase in the number of huge factory ships which are able to stay at sea for weeks at a time. At least twenty of the world's most important fisheries have disappeared in the last 25 years with many more suffering so badly from overfishing that they are unlikely to recover.

As catches have gradually become smaller, so the mesh sizes used in fishing nets have decreased, allowing smaller and smaller fish to be caught. Fishing using nets is indiscriminate. Any fish too big to get through the mesh will be caught. For every one tonne of prawns caught, three tonnes of fish are needlessly killed and thrown away. 20,000 porpoises die each year in the nets of salmon fishing boats in the Atlantic and Pacific Oceans and tens of thousands of dolphins are killed each year by tuna fishermen.

Commercial fishing

Some fish, called pelagic fish, live in the upper parts of the water and are caught by drift netting. This involves suspending a net from floats stretched between two boats so that fish swim into it. Once caught in the net the fish cannot escape unless they are small enough to fit through the net's mesh.
Fish that live deeper in the water, the mid and bottom-feeders, are caught by trawling. This involves dragging a large net through the water, catching whatever happens to be in the way. The size of the holes in the net is again very important and it is vital for the conservation of fish stocks that nets with a very small mesh are banned as they catch young fish before they have become sufficiently mature to reproduce.

There are numerous examples of how overfishing can seriously affect not only the fish stocks but also the livelihoods of the fishermen. A delicate balance needs to be struck between catching large numbers of fish so as to make a commercial living and ensuring that there are enough fish left alive to be able to replenish stocks for future years. Disputes have occurred between countries. For example, a serious dispute took place between British and Icelandic fishermen over the Icelandic cod fisheries. British trawlers continued to fish for cod despite a ban on fishing put in effect by the Icelandic government. There were confrontations between British and Icelandic trawlers which became known as the 'Cod War'. There is now a 100-mile exclusion zone around Iceland in which foreign vessels are not allowed to fish. As a result Icelandic cod stocks are starting to improve, though it is unlikely that they will ever recover fully.

Effects of overfishing on other wildlife

The overfishing of a particular species has 'knock-on' effects along the food chain. For example, as herring is eaten by cod, if herring are overfished, the cod population suffers as well. The sandeel is the main food supply for seabirds such as the puffin. Sandeels have been fished around the Shetland Islands since the mid-1970's. As a result colonies of seabirds nesting around Shetland have declined with some even failing to breed for several years.

In the Antarctic, fishing for krill is threatening to disrupt the delicate balance of nature in these waters. Krill are small shrimps and are a very important trophic level in the food chain. They are the main source of food for the great whales, and also supplement the diets of seals, penguins, squid and fish. Krill occur in huge swarms many miles across. Since the 1980's six countries, including Japan and Russia, have been harvesting krill. The natural balance in the Antarctic has already been upset by the overexploitation of whales; the heavy fishing of krill will undoubtedly have a serious effect on the populations of animals that feed on them.

Is there a solution?

There have been dramatic increases in the intensity and efficiency of commercial fishing methods. This has resulted in **over-fishing** in many areas of the world. At present short-term economic pressures are preventing sensible long-term planning for a sustainable yield. Fish are an example of a renewable resource. Over-fishing results in a depletion of younger fish so that the 'breeding stock' is unable to maintain previous population levels. If the rate at which they are removed exceeds that at which they have been produced their supply is ultimately exhausted. Fish are not generally farmed. Humans remove them from the seas with no attempt to replace stocks by breeding.

International agreement has been reached on controls such as:
- Imposing quotas on catches based on scientific estimates of the size of the fish stocks.
- Restricting the mesh size of nets. Correct mesh size should be used in all nets to ensure that fish of the correct age are caught and to prevent as much as possible 'accidental' catches of other fish. Larger mesh nets allow juvenile fish to escape and so survive to reproduce.
- International agreements limiting catches are necessary to safeguard fish stocks for the use not only of humans but for marine life as well.
- Enforcing closed seasons for fishing.
- Enforcing exclusion zones.

The European Commission has successfully banned the fishing of particular species. This measure enables the breeding stocks to recover. Legislation limiting the size of fishing fleets, restricting the numbers of days spent at sea, and controlling the mesh size of nets has been less successful as they are difficult to enforce. This is because commercial fishermen naturally resist attempts to limit their income or their job prospects.

Fish farming

On the face of it, fish farming, or aquaculture, seems like a practical solution to the problem of overfishing. In the UK trout and salmon are the fish most commonly farmed. Fish can be bred and grown to maturity in ponds, lakes and managed enclosures in estuaries, where predation is reduced and food supplies are maintained. For plankton-feeders the growth of phytoplankton can be aided by the addition of artificial fertilizers to the water. Fish grow rapidly when they are reared in the warm waters discharged from factories.

The true cost of fish farming

Fish farming, however, is the cause of many problems. Public demand for cheaper food means that farmed salmon are often kept, for financial reasons, very densely stocked, with huge numbers of fish crammed into very little space. In this state the fish can more easily become diseased and these diseases can spread to wild fish. Huge amounts of antibiotics are required to keep the fish moderately healthy. The pesticides used to control fish parasites are also known to harm marine invertebrates. There is also the likelihood that the delicate balance of the waterways may be upset. For example, eutrophication can result when fish excreta, waste food and fertilizer is carried in the water to the wider community around the rearing pens.

Is organic fish sustainable?

When fish escape the farmed fish interbreed with wild fish and potentially weaken wild stocks. There is also the problem of pollution in the water and seabed around fish farms. Farmed salmon, which are carnivorous, eat three times their body weight in fish feed, which is made from other fish. This is not the best use of resources from an environmental point of view. Another problem with all salmon (wild or farmed) is that they can contain high levels of dioxins and polychlorinated biphenyls (PCBs). Farmed fish, labelled as 'organic', are not immune to the problems of fish farming, as their feed, although organic, is just as unsustainable as non-organic feed. It is of little surprise that farmed fish all too often have poor texture and flavour.

Effects of human activities on the carbon cycle

Carbon cycle

Carbon dioxide is added to the air by the respiration of animals, plants and microorganisms and by the combustion of fossil fuels. Photosynthesis takes place on so great a scale that it re-uses on a daily basis almost as much carbon dioxide as is released into the atmosphere. This is the basis of the carbon cycle. The production of carbohydrates, proteins and fats contributes to plant growth and subsequently to animal growth through complex food webs. The dead remains of both plants and animals are then acted upon by saprobionts in the soil which ultimately release gaseous CO_2 back to the atmosphere.
In past times large quantities of dead organisms accumulated in anaerobic conditions and so were prevented from decaying. In time they formed coal, oil and other fossil fuels. The burning of these fuels returns more CO_2 to the atmosphere and has resulted in a rise in CO_2 in the atmosphere, particularly over the last 50 years.

❑ **Action**   Draw a labelled diagram of the carbon cycle linking the processes of photosynthesis, respiration, decomposition, fossilisation and combustion.

Humans and the carbon cycle

There are two main reasons for the increase:
1. **The burning of fossil fuels.** This accounts for about 70% of the increase in CO_2, most (76%) coming from industrialised countries.
2. **Deforestation** – accounts for about 30% of the increased CO_2 levels, as about half the world's forests have been removed over the last 30 years.
   Forests help to maintain the balance of carbon dioxide and oxygen in the atmosphere. This is important because carbon dioxide is a 'greenhouse gas'. It absorbs radiation from the Earth and if it is allowed to accumulate it leads to 'global warming'.

Other greenhouse gases include CFC's, which have been used as aerosol propellants and as coolants in fridges and freezers and nitrous oxides, which are emitted from vehicle exhausts and methane. The amount of these greenhouse gases in the environment is known to be rising. **Carbon dioxide** is particularly important in the greenhouse effect because it represents about 49% of all greenhouse gases.

'Greenhouse gases' form a layer in the atmosphere acting like glass in a greenhouse. Greenhouse gases allow high-energy solar radiation to pass through to the Earth's surface. Much of this energy is 'bounced back' towards space as heat but some of the energy is absorbed and trapped by the greenhouse gases. The greenhouse effect is a natural process without which the average temperature on Earth would be too low to sustain life. Since the Industrial Revolution there has been a gradual build-up of these gases and this has increased the greenhouse effect. In recent years the situation has become much worse due to the increase in industrialisation in countries such as China, and the increase in global transport.

This increase in greenhouse gases is thought to be the cause of **global warming**.

Global warming

Global warming refers to an average increase in the Earth's temperature, which in turn causes changes in climate. A warmer Earth may lead to changes in rainfall patterns, a rise in sea level, and a wide range of impacts on plants, wildlife, and humans. When scientists talk about the issue of climate change, their concern is about global warming caused by human activities.

A number of predictions have been made regarding the severity of global warming. It is suggested that if concentrations of greenhouse gases rise at current rates, possible temperature increases during the next 50 years could be in the range 1.5 – 5.5°C.

Possible consequence of global warming may be:

✓ Some melting of polar icecaps resulting in flooding in coastal areas.

✓ Increased frequency of droughts, hurricanes and cyclones, and also forest fires.

✓ In tropical areas of the world decreased availability of water might lead to the formation of deserts.

✓ Increased crop yields, but insect pest populations might also increase.

Climate change will have serious effects on world food production with massive reductions in the grain crops of North America and Central Asia. This would have serious economic and political consequences. Governments agree that there is a link between greenhouse gas concentrations and global warming and there have been a number of international conferences discussing the issue. The most important is the **Kyoto agreement.** The protocol was agreed on 11 December 1997 at the 3rd Conference of the Parties to the treaty when they met in Kyoto, and came into force on 16 February 2005.

In February 2007 the European Union agreed a pact to slash greenhouse gas emissions by 20% within 13 years unilaterally and also pledged to push for an agreement with the US and other industrialised countries to cut them by 30% by the same deadline. European environment ministers made the target for 2020 binding on all 27 EU countries, but are yet to agree on how to "share the burden" of combating climate change, with countries such as Britain and Germany promising large cuts whereas other high-growth but less developed countries are allowed more leeway. British officials, hailing the agreement as "an historic milestone," said the aim was to reach a deal on "burden-sharing" before the G8 summit of industrialised countries, including Russia, in Heiligendamm in Germany, in June 2007. "Our commitment to a 30% cut [on 1990 levels] as part of a global agreement strengthens the EU's ability to lead the debate at the G8 and UN climate change talks and to secure an ambitious outcome," David Miliband, environment secretary, said. The targets are due to be endorsed by the EU's spring summit when heads of government will press emerging economies such as China to join in.

❏ **Action** Check the web to find out if there have been any recent developments.

Carbon footprint

The term 'carbon footprint' owes its origins to the idea that a footprint is what has been left behind as a result of an individual's activities. There are two possible ways of 'tracing' a carbon footprint:

- The carbon footprint can be seen as the total amount of carbon dioxide and other greenhouse gases emitted over the full life cycle of a **product or service**. Usually a carbon footprint is expressed as a CO_2 equivalent (usually in kilogrammes or tonnes), which accounts for the same global warming effects of different greenhouse gases.

- An alternative definition of carbon footprint is the total amount of carbon dioxide attributable to the actions of an **individual** (mainly through their energy use) over a period of one year. This definition forms the basis of the personal carbon calculators. Individual carbon footprints can be either:

✓ direct emissions (typically from energy used in the home and in transport, including travel by cars, planes, rail and other public transport)

✓ indirect emissions , including CO_2 emissions as a result of goods and services consumed.

Global warming and climate change may require new crops to be developed by genetic engineering.

Global warming and climate change will undoubtedly affect the distribution of species and are a possible cause of extinction. It may be necessary to develop, through genetic engineering, drought resistant crops. The following article shows the scientists are already making headway in this area of research.

Extract from ABC news Online

Gene find may produce drought-resistant crops By Julia Limb for The World Today

Australian scientists have made a significant breakthrough in genetic research which could lead to the development of drought-resistant crops and save farmers hundreds of millions of dollars. In research to be published in leading international journal *Nature*, the scientists from the Australian National University report that they have identified a gene which regulates water efficiency in plants. It is the first time such a gene has been isolated and scientists say it will allow them to improve the drought resistance of most crop species and could have major implications for crops grown in dry areas.

The laboratory plant *Arabidopsis*, from the canola family, is the only species other than rice which has had its genome fully sequenced. The new gene, called erecta, is the first of three genes believed to control water efficiency in plants to be identified. Josette Masle from the Research School of Biological Sciences led the research and she says the discovery of the gene will have major implications.

"This is especially significant if you are in high altitude environments where water is limited and need plants that use as little water as possible," Dr Masle said."The gene we found is a gene that affects how much water plants lose."Dr Masle says the discovery will now allow her team to look for the same gene in other crop species.

"We know that many species carry a gene with a similar sequence to the one we have identified in arabidopsis," she said."Those species include key crops for Australia, and crops such as wheat, barley, rice, canola and tomatoes in many other parts of the world.

The findings have also given researchers at the CSIRO a major boost."It's a very, very significant finding worldwide, not just for Australia where water limits crop growth, but water is a major issue globally for future food production," chief research scientist Richard Richards said."So it's a very significant finding when you put it in a global context." Dr Richards says his group, which has already released two varieties of drought-resistant wheat, now has a new molecular tool for developing other water efficient crops.

"What this new finding is going to help us do is to be more efficient to make those selections," he said."So it may reduce the amount of time it takes for us to release a variety. It's a very long process, it often takes about 10 years so if you can reduce the time just by one year, which is in fact a very significant amount, that's going to speed up the whole process. It's also going to enable researchers right around the world to focus more specifically on water-use efficiency as well."

Dr Richards says the identification of this gene will have an important role not just for developing crops using conventional methods. "We have the potential to move almost straight away using conventional means," he said. "When GM is more acceptable, we'll be able to just turn the volume of these genes up a little bit more and improve the efficiency of water use and drought resistance."

Nitrogen containing fertilizers

The harvesting of crops removes mineral elements and cropping interrupts the natural recycling of nutrients. Nutrients lost can be replaced by the addition of natural organic waste materials such as manure or compost or by adding artificial or inorganic fertilizers. Most fertilizers are used to supply the elements nitrogen, phosphorous and potassium. The use of fertilizers has contributed to increased productivity and has enabled new, poorer, areas of land to be used for agriculture. However, the over-use of fertilizers has led to environmental problems. Minerals intended for the crop may be washed into waterways, encouraging the growth of algae and so contribute to the process of eutrophication.

Problems caused by nitrate-containing fertilizers

As the human population has increased, people's expectations to have plentiful, high quality food has risen. Agricultural practises have had to change in an attempt to meet the demands. In developed countries agriculture has become more intensive, providing high yields of crops from relatively small areas of land. However, this increase in food production has had a deleterious effect on the environment. One example of the potential conflicts between the use of the environment to produce food and conservation of the environment is in the use of fertilizers for farming. The increased use of nitrate-containing fertilizers has had some harmful effects on both aquatic and terrestrial ecosystems.

- Problems caused by excess nitrate in soils.

On agricultural land the increased use of fertilizer has reduced species diversity on grassland. Fertilizers increase the growth of grasses and plants such as nettles which shade out smaller plants.

- Problems caused by nitrates leaching into rivers.

Eutrophication is a natural process during which the concentration of salts builds up in bodies of water. In lakes and rivers the salts normally accumulate until an equilibrium is reached where they are exactly counterbalanced by the rate at which they are removed. The salts necessary for eutrophication of lakes and rivers are largely nitrates and phosphates. The leaching of these salts from the surrounding land is a slow, natural process. However, sewage and fertilizers are an additional source of these salts.

Nitrate is highly soluble and is readily leached from soil and washed into rivers from surrounding land. The first effect may be an **algal bloom** where the waters become densely populated with species of algae, their growth being enhanced by abundant nutrients. At this stage the water may become green and light is unable to penetrate to any depth.

The plants in the deeper regions of the lake are unable to photosynthesise and therefore die. There is a general decrease in animal species diversity as they rely on the plants for food and shelter. The short lived algae soon die and are decomposed by saprobiontic bacteria which use a lot of oxygen creating a biochemical oxygen demand (BOD). The water in all but the very upper layers becomes deoxygenated, so that fish and other oxygen-requiring species die. In the final stages of the process of eutrophication anaerobic bacteria in the water may reduce nitrate to nitrite (both nitrate and nitrite are toxic compounds). In view of their toxicity, the EU has set a limit of 11.3 parts per million(ppm) total nitrogen in drinking water. This figure has been exceeded in parts of the UK.

The indiscriminate use of nitrogen-containing fertilizers may pollute water supplies and pose a threat to human health.

Measures to reduce problems

Where the problem of high nitrate levels in waterways is particularly serious farmers must comply with strict legislation to reduce the quantity of nitrate they release into the environment. They must:

- ✓ Restrict the amount of fertilizer applied to the soil.
- ✓ Only apply fertilizer at a time when the crops are actively growing.
- ✓ Leave a strip at least 10 metres wide next to watercourses.

Drainage ditches

Farmers plough land to improve aeration of the soil. This enables the process of nitrification by aerobic nitrifying bacteria to produce nitrates to take place. Farmland also requires good drainage. Digging drainage ditches has a detrimental effect on habitats. Historically, the greatest decline has occurred through agricultural intensification, afforestation, and commercial peat extraction.

There has been a dramatic decline in the area of lowland raised bog habitat in the past 100 years. The area of lowland raised bog in the UK retaining a largely undisturbed surface is estimated to have diminished by around 94% from an original 95,000 ha to 6,000 ha, with only 500 ha remaining in England. Future decline is likely to be the result of the gradual desiccation of bogs damaged by a range of drainage activities and/or a general lowering of groundwater tables.

Rare and localised invertebrates, such as the Large heath butterfly *(Coenonympha tullia)*, the Bog bush cricket (*Metrioptera brachyptera*) and Mire pill beetle (*Curimopsis nigrita*) are found on some lowland raised bog sites.

- ✓ **Peat extraction**
  Removal of peat in existing and proposed new areas
- ✓ **Landfill development**
  Use of cut-over bogs for landfill.
- ✓ **Afforestation**
  Trees (and associated furrows) dry out neighbouring areas and act as an invasive seed source.
- ✓ **Drainage**
  Neighbouring agricultural areas require lowered water levels via marginal ring-ditches and other intrusive drainage measures. Drying out the raised bog through drainage allows invasion by scrub and trees which in turn speed up the drying out process and lead to the loss of special habitat and fauna.
- ✓ **Water abstraction**
  Abstraction of water within the catchment area will have an adverse effect on the hydrology of a raised bog.
- ✓ **Pollution**
  Run-off from agricultural land (fertilizers and pesticides) will damage the ecology of the bog.
- ✓ **Livestock & game management**
  Drainage, trampling, burning, contamination with feed and droppings.
- ✓ **Built development (roads etc)**
  Apart from direct impact, the natural hydrology is disrupted.

Biofuels

What are biofuels?

Biofuels are any kind of fuel that is biological in origin. They exist in a variety of forms including wood, wood chippings and straw: biogas (methane) from animals' excrement; ethanol, diesel or other liquid fuels made from processing plant material or waste oil.

Ethanol for fuel is made through fermentation, the same process which produces it in wine and beer. Biodiesel is an oil substitute manufactured from oil seed rape. Biogas, mainly methane, is used on a small scale to power generators.

In recent years, the term "biofuel" has come to mean ethanol and diesel made from crops including corn, sugarcane and rapeseed.

Bio-ethanol, an alcohol, is usually mixed with petrol, while biodiesel is either used on its own or in a mixture.

Are biofuels climate-friendly?

In principle, biofuels are a way of reducing greenhouse gas emissions compared to conventional transport fuels. Burning the fuels releases carbon dioxide; but growing the plants absorbs a comparable amount of the gas from the atmosphere. However, energy is used in farming and processing the crops, and this can make biofuels as polluting as petroleum-based fuels, depending on what is grown and how it is treated. A recent UK government publication declared that biofuels reduced emissions "by 50-60% compared to fossil fuels".

Where are biofuels used?

Production of ethanol doubled globally between 2000 and 2005, with biodiesel output quadrupling. Brazil leads the world in production and use, making about 16 billion litres per year of ethanol from its sugarcane industry. Sixty percent of new cars can run on a fuel mix which includes 85% ethanol. The European Union has a target for 2010 that 5.75% of transport fuels should come from biological sources, but the target is unlikely to be met. The British government's Renewable Transport Fuel Obligation requires 5% of the fuel sold at the pump by 2010 to be biofuel. In the US, the Renewable Fuels Standard aims to double the use of biofuels in transport by 2012.

What are the downsides?

From the environmental point of the view, the big issue is biodiversity. With much of the western world's farmland already consisting of fields of monocultured crops, the fear is that a major adoption of biofuels will reduce habitat for animals and wild plants still further. Asian countries may be tempted to replace rainforest with more palm oil plantations. If increased proportions of food crops such as corn or soy are used for fuel, that may push prices up, affecting food supplies for less prosperous populations. The mixed picture regarding the climate benefit of biofuels leads some observers to say that the priority should be reducing energy use; they claim that initiatives on biofuels detract attention from this and are more of a financial help to politically important farming lobbies than a serious attempt to cut greenhouse gas emissions.

There are also a few technical problems. Although engines can generally cope with the new fuels, current technologies limit production, because only certain parts of specific plants can be used. The tough cellulose has to be pre-treated before it can be fermented. It is hoped that the so-called second-generation of biofuels will process the cellulose found in many plants. This should lead to far more efficient production using a much greater range of plants and plant waste.

The following was reported in the 'Guardian' August 2007.

Biofuels switch a mistake say the researchers.

Increasing production of biofuels to combat climate change will release between two and nine times more carbon gases over the next 30 years than fossil fuels, according to the first comprehensive analysis of emissions from biofuels.

Biofuels - petrol and diesel extracted from plants - are presented as an environmentally friendly alternative to fossil fuels because the crops absorb carbon dioxide from the atmosphere as they grow.

The study warns that forests must not be cleared to make way for biofuel crops. Clearing forests produces an immediate release of carbon gases into the atmosphere, accompanied by a loss of habitats, wildlife and livelihoods, the researchers said.

Britain is committed to substituting 10% of its transport fuel with biofuels under European plans to slash carbon emissions by 2020.

"Biofuel policy is rushing ahead without understanding the implications," said Renton Righelato of the World Land Trust, a conservation charity. "It is a mistake in climate change terms to use biofuels."

Dr Righelato's study, with Dominick Spracklen from the University of Leeds, is the first to calculate the impact of biofuel carbon emissions across the whole cycle of planting, extraction and conversion into fuel. They report in the journal *Science* that between two and nine times more carbon emissions are avoided by trapping carbon in trees and forest soil than by replacing fossil fuels with biofuels.

Around 40% of Europe's agricultural land would be needed to grow biofuel crops to meet the 10% fossil fuel substitution target. That demand on arable land cannot be met in the EU or the US, say the scientists, so is likely to shift the burden on land in developing countries.

The National Farmers Union said 20% of Britain's agricultural land could be used to grow biofuels by 2010. However, the researchers say reforesting the land would be a better way to reduce emissions.

Biofuels look good in climate change terms from a Western perspective, said Dr Spracklen, but globally they actually lead to higher carbon emissions. "Brazil, Paraguay, Indonesia among others have huge deforestation programmes to supply the world biofuel market", he said.

The researchers say the emphasis should be placed on increasing the efficiency of fossil fuel use and moving to carbon-free alternatives such as renewable energy.

Decision making

Increased human pressures on the environment

Ecology is the study of how living organisms interact with each other and with the environment. Although humans have existed on Earth for a relatively short period of time they have had a far greater influence on the environment than any other species. The study of ecology is vital in order to collect data about the environment and how it is changing. Decisions have to be made based on the data, so the data have to be accurate and reliable. People need to be well informed in order to make important decisions that may have consequences for future generations.

It is vital that the course of action taken is based on the following principles.
There is a need:

- for environmental monitoring and the need to provide data which is reliable and valid.
- to consider the issues surrounding the collection of data.
- to consider the possibility of conflicting evidence and interpretation.
- to recognise the possible tentative nature of conclusions.
- to achieve sustainability by changes in human attitudes and to make informed choices.
- for political decision-making to be informed by knowledge based on sound scientific principles.